D0378952

JGV

AUBERGE DE L'ILL
les Frères HAEBERLIN

Home Cooking with Jean-Georges:
My Favorite Simple Recipes
(with Genevieve Ko)

Asian Flavors of Jean-Georges
(with Genevieve Ko)

Simple to Spectacular:
How to Take One Basic Recipe to Four Levels
    of Sophistication
(with Mark Bittman)

Jean-Georges:
Cooking at Home with a Four-Star Chef
(with Mark Bittman)

Simple Cuisine:
The Easy, New Approach to Four-Star Cooking

JEAN-GEORGES VONGERICHTEN

with **MICHAEL RUHLMAN**

W. W. NORTON & COMPANY
Independent Publishers Since 1923

JGV

A LIFE IN 12 RECIPES

Drawings made by Jean-Georges Vongerichten are on pages iii, 64, 80, 108, 148, 172, 196, 206.
Photos on pages 2, 18, 38, 50, 124, 136, 164, and 274 are from Jean-Georges Vongerichten.
Photograph on page 136 is from Lois Freedman.
Photograph on page 274 is from Daniel Del Vecchio.

For information about permission to reproduce selections from this book, write to Permissions, W. W. Norton & Company, Inc., 500 Fifth Avenue, New York, NY 10110

For information about special discounts for bulk purchases, please contact W. W. Norton Special Sales at specialsales@wwnorton.com or 800-233-4830

Manufacturing by Lake Book
Book design by Lovedog Studio
Production manager: Anna Oler

ISBN 978-0-393-60848-9

W. W. Norton & Company, Inc.
500 Fifth Avenue, New York, N.Y. 10110
www.wwnorton.com

W. W. Norton & Company Ltd.
15 Carlisle Street, London W1D 3BS

1 2 3 4 5 6 7 8 9 0

I would like to thank the city of New York, my adopted city, and its people for supporting me for the past thirty-three years and allowing me to fulfill my dreams.

Good food is the foundation of genuine happiness.

—AUGUSTE ESCOFFIER

CONTENTS

PART V:
BECOMING A CHEF-RESTAURATEUR   163

THE
APPRENTICE

PART I

With my mom and dad enjoying a cocktail in summer.
We had a lovely patio where we ate our meals. The
year is about 1988, on a visit home from New York,
where I was chef of Lafayette in the Drake hotel.

1.

LISTEN TO YOUR CHILDHOOD

YOU ARE STARTING OUT AND ASKING YOURSELF HOW TO proceed in this world of cooking, or *if* to proceed in this world. What path to follow? What does it mean to be a cook and a chef? What, you wonder, do you need to know? I'm asked all the time, "How did *you* do it?" This question isn't easily answered. But my hope is that my story, how I got to where I am, my evolution as a cook and then a chef, might help you answer those questions for yourself.

I didn't know I wanted to spend my life cooking. I was an aimless country boy from Alsace, a region of flatlands in easternmost France. The Black Forest and the German border were five miles away, and I grew up speaking not French but, rather, Alsatian, a German patois (I wouldn't learn French until age five, when I began school). I liked to have fun. We lived in a house my great-grandparents had built in 1833; it had a river on one side and woods on the other. Me, my two younger brothers and older sister, my parents, my grandparents, two aunts and their kids, all in the same house. The house was big, so I was lucky to have my own room, but still, it was a crowded household. We were on top of one another.

My family owned a coal business. Our coal came down the river on barges. My parents worked hard. My dad sold coal and wood. He drove the delivery trucks. He did everything, from delivering fuel to collecting bills to entertaining clients. He would even go into the forests to get the wood, which would have to dry for a year before it could be sold. But their biggest struggle by far, a never-ending problem, was getting people to pay. They were always chasing after clients. Even my mom would go through the town knocking on doors to get money. I think maybe that's why I do the work I do. People have to pay me before they leave. Honestly, that remains one of the great things about the restaurant business, not having to chase down customers as my mother was continually doing.

The other lesson I learned, I see now, was to *not* do your business where you live. My parents' work never left them. They would get calls in the middle of the night from people saying their heating had gone out. So my father had to go to them to make sure they had heat in the middle of a frigid night. Me, when I leave the restaurant, I leave my work behind. I suppose I could get a call at midnight saying there's a fire in the kitchen. But even then I'd be able to say, "Call 911!" This work is so intense and so constant, the capacity to turn it off is fundamental to your being able to restore yourself for the day to come.

As a boy, I was carefree. I had a wonderful childhood. I played in the woods and climbed the mountains of coal behind our house. My whole childhood I was black with soot.

Throughout my childhood and youth, perhaps tellingly, the kitchen was the busiest part of our house. My mother, who was twenty-two when I was born, in 1957, cooked. As I noted, ours was a packed household, just with the immediate family alone. But not only were we three generations under one roof, we also had a number of employees working for our business there. They would need to be fed. And clients would always be invited to meals, as well. This meant that every day, we had a three-course lunch for around forty people. My mother had lunch on the table at twelve-thirty sharp. Dinner appeared at seven-thirty. Sharp. Every day. Looking back, this stays with me. Her rigorous schedule. Lunch, twelve-thirty, every day, every week, all year long. It never varied, and she was never late. Dinner: seven-thirty. Period.

Lunch in France was the big meal, but for us, even dinner was big—typically twenty people for dinner. Imagine it if you can. Every day, lunch for forty, dinner for twenty. It was a mini restaurant. When I look back on it now, I understand that I basically grew up in a restaurant doing sixty covers every day—about the same number of seats I have at my restaurant Jean-Georges—and I watched the whole process each day of my childhood. I absorbed the preparation, the attention to timing, the organization needed to get that much food, prepare it, and serve it for that many people.

My mother didn't work alone, of course; everyone helped. But she was the chef—the head of the kitchen. When I was a child, I didn't cook, though I watched the whole production. Everybody waking up early in the morning, peeling potatoes. That was my benchmark—everyone worked.

Eventually, at around age ten or eleven, when I could reach the counter, I worked as well. I learned my mother's palate, which was impeccable. Nothing ever needed salt. She made things bright with aggressive acidity—which, you'll notice, remains one of the keystones of my cooking and seasoning. And by the time I was age twelve or so, she would have me taste for seasoning because I was so good at it. Soon I developed a palate more nuanced than hers.

I learned from my mother how to hustle. My father was more laid-back, but not my mother. He was over six feet tall and she was much shorter, but she was the dynamo.

Her food was simple but very, very good, and she always used the best-quality ingredients. Quality, quality, quality. I grew up with that—it was the norm. If we had chicken for dinner, it was from Bresse. The leg of lamb was from the Pyrenees. The goose was local. Forty of my most favorite meals come from my mother. The *baeckeoffe* in our household was a layering of potatoes, carrots, and leeks, alternating with meat—bacon, beef, usually plenty of pork, whatever inexpensive cuts were available from the butcher—so that there were three layers of vegetables, two of meat. The sauerkraut was fabulous. We fermented it in the cellar, and she would cook it with goose fat and onions, an hour and a half, that was it, so that it was still crunchy and fresh.

Even her boiled cauliflower was amazing. She'd use the cooking water to make a kind of béchamel sauce. This was ingenious in its practicality—she never threw away flavor. She'd make a roux, then add the cauliflower water till she had a thick sauce. Then she'd whip in crème fraîche and egg yolk—I wouldn't learn the term "liaison" for years, but this was what she was doing, enriching the sauce with egg yolk and fat, a technique that gives sauces extraordinary silkiness. She could serve the cauliflower just like that, with the sauce alone, or she could sauce it, cover it with grated Gruyère, and gratin it. And that would be the centerpiece of a meal, served with soft-boiled eggs and potatoes. We had that once a week.

When she roasted a chicken, she made a sauce for it right there in the pan, with water and wine. She would never make a stock. And I don't think canned broth was available, but even if it had been, she wouldn't have used it. Flavor doesn't come out of a can. It comes out of the food. Water is all you need.

She made salads every day. Greens, cucumber, shallots, crème fraîche, always very acidic. She used a special vinegar native to the region called Melfor vinegar, made with wine, herbs, and fermented honey. All her salads were like, *Bang!* The celery rémoulade had a *lot* of mustard, a *lot* of vinegar. Delicious, and good for the digestion. For dessert, a *fromage blanc* tart or a tart-cherry clafouti.

And while so much of her food was traditional, she was open to new ideas and being creative. She was the first person I knew to use olive oil, for instance, which was hard to come by in Alsace.

Also important to me, though, was what she *didn't* eat: leftovers. She would never offer or eat leftover food. Only food cooked that day. And I am the same way. I can't do it. The other weekend I cooked for about twenty people at my home. I made lobster. (The lobsters were so, so good. I put them all in a big aluminum pan with butter and fresh herbs, sealed it, then poked a lot of holes in the pan and put it on a hot grill; that way, the lobsters steam but they also pick up great smoke from the fire.) I had maybe fifteen lobster tail halves left over the next day. We weren't going to throw them away, so we made lobster rolls. Everyone else ate them. I couldn't. Just couldn't do it. It must come from watching her.

But perhaps her most important influence on me, on my cooking, I must reiterate, was the high acidity, something I love to this day. It is one of the most fundamental elements of my cooking, one of the keys that set me apart in New York in the 1980s—and I learned it from her. A sauce must be three times as powerfully flavored as the meat you're serving it with. I learned promptness—twelve-thirty, seven-thirty, every day. I learned hard work and organization. I learned how to work with other people in a kitchen. I learned economy in feeding large numbers of people. Never discount what your home and your family give you. Listen to your childhood.

My mother is now eighty-four. She still drives, still makes fourteen pounds of foie gras to give away at Christmastime. (For me, foie gras will always be a food reserved for this holiday.) She still goes to buy a fresh baguette every day.

I love all the food of Alsace. Her rich goose stew, for instance. She made this a lot. In Alsace, the geese were big and fat. She removed the skin, marinated the goose overnight in white wine and herbs. She browned the goose, browned the onions and vegetables. She'd add the white wine along with the marinade and lots of pepper. Cook it till it was falling off the bone. And that was it. She served it with braised cabbage and spaetzle. It was so delicious. Probably the best goose stew I've had anywhere. Perhaps because I'd been eating it my whole life, I never paused to consider what made her goose stew different. I'd long been a chef before I thought to ask, "*Maman,* what do you thicken it with?" I knew that she braised it in water and wine, only no matter how long you cook it, that sauce will always be thin. But when hers reached the table, the liquid had a lovely, saucelike texture.

"Coffee," she told me.

This was a revelation. I was already a chef at a three-star restaurant when I learned this; I ran a place that relied on long-simmered, roasted bones. While she usually relied on water, when she had more flavorful ingredients at hand, she would use them, use all she could for flavor. There was always leftover coffee in the pot, so she mixed this cold coffee with flour to make a coffee slurry. And this was what she used to thicken the cooking liquid. It gave such amazing flavors to the stew. I couldn't believe it.

This was where my interest in coffee-flavored sauces with meat came from. Later, I would use this idea—coffee and chicory—for many dishes. When there were coffee shortages in our town after the war, my parents used a lot of chicory, a plant in the dandelion family whose root can be roasted and ground to make a kind of coffee. So I grew up with chicory as well. When I began cooking on my own, I would steep chicory in water and strain the liquid, which was darker than espresso. I'd add onion puree to balance the bitterness, mount butter into this, season it with salt and pepper. That's it. Perfect for steak, as anyone familiar with American red-eye gravy knows. For me, the idea began with my mother's goose stew.

So this was my youth, in a busy restaurant-like kitchen serving the food of my region: goose, and warm potato salad, and sauerkraut—all of it with lots and lots of acidity. Breakfasts were simple: coffee and a piece of bread (when I was young I got fresh farm milk mixed with Ovaltine—or Ovomaltine, as we called it). Eggs were for lunch and dinner, never breakfast. (I never had an egg for breakfast until I came to America, and now I like them sunny-side up for breakfast, eating all the whites first and saving the delicious, runny yolks for last.) All those hundreds upon hundreds of lunches and dinners for a great household of people—that was how I grew up.

Sundays were different. Sundays were the day off. Saturday night, *Maman* would make the dough for *kougelhopf*, a German-Alsatian Bundt cake with a brioche-like texture, even though it doesn't include any eggs. That would be cooked the next morning for breakfast before church. For dinner, my father, Georges, cooked. He was a *good* cook, too. He did the fancy meals, things like roasted pheasant and truffle-stuffed chicken and lamb gigot. While we went to church, he stayed home to make elaborate meals for the family on my mother's day off from cooking. He was creative in the kitchen and loved cooking, although really, I think he just wanted to avoid going to Mass and he used the fancy Sunday meal as an excuse to get out of it.

When I look back on my youth, and where my first formative cooking memories come from, I see that they come not from elaborate Sunday and holiday meals, and not from my earliest lessons under Monsieur Paul, the chef of the first restaurant I worked in, Auberge de l'Ill. The daily cooking for a big family, employees, and clients is what informs all my cooking today. Every day at twelve-thirty and seven-thirty, without fail. My mother's cooking and her hustling in the kitchen to feed for all those people every day.

When I began cooking at Auberge, I was very excited by all I was learning, about stocks, about sauces. So when I returned home on weekends, I was eager to show off what I knew. "Here, *Maman*," I would say, "let me show you how to do it." But when she heard what I wanted her to do, she told me I was crazy. She said, "What am I going to do? Make stock at eight in the morning? That's ridiculous. I have things to do. I cook *à la minute*, the way I feel. I start cooking at eleven-thirty. You come to the table at twelve-thirty. I'm not making a fumet."

And you know, she was right. I would one day, as I'm about to tell you, go on to work in Michelin-starred restaurants, work under masterful chefs, open restaurants all over the world, make my name in New York by running restaurants serving all kinds of cuisines. But to this day, to know myself, I look to these memories of home, of childhood, and the lessons I learned from my mother about economy, simplicity, ingenuity, and her powerful hand with the salt and the vinegar—they guide me still.

Jeanine Vongerichten's Goose Stew

This is the exact goose stew from my childhood, the goose stew I grew up with and still cherish. It's so good it makes me long for home. In Alsace, goose wasn't a once-a-year holiday meal, the way it is here—goose stew was served all winter long. It's a generous meal. The geese there were much bigger than they are in the United States. If I showed an American goose to my mother today, she'd say, "What is that? It looks like reindeer." Too lean, and too small. Our geese were old and took several hours of braising to become tender. They had abundant fat, twice as thick as American geese, and *Maman* would render it all down on the stove top and have two big jars of cooking fat to flavor the sauerkraut with.

I break the goose down into ten pieces, a lot like a traditional Escoffier chicken sauté. Leg and thigh, breast halves with the wing still attached. That's a great technique for all kinds of poultry dishes; I love it. Here, however, I remove the wing drumette from the breast but leave lots of breast meat attached, so that each wing is enough for a whole portion. Also notice how every piece is left on the bone. This helps the meat retain its structure and results in juicy breast pieces.

1 eight- to ten-pound goose

Break the goose down by first removing the legs from the body: slice between the breast and the leg and snap the thigh toward you to pop it out of its ball joint. Then cut through along the backbone to capture all the meat. Remove the skin and fat from these pieces and set it aside. Separate the drumsticks from the thighs by slicing through the line of fat that runs directly over the joint. For a very clean presentation, cut the end off the drumstick as well.

Next remove the two end segments of the wings (the tips and flats), leaving only the drumette attached to the carcass. Slice into the fat end of the breast in a broad circle above the wing joint to remove the wing drumette. The idea is to take plenty of breast meat off with the drumette, as you separate the wing from the carcass, to make this a decent serving portion. Do the same with the other wing drumette. Remove the skin and fat from these pieces and combine it with the other skin and fat. Take the ends off these drumettes as you did with the legs for a clean presentation.

Stand the goose on end, neck side down, and slice through the rib cage just below the meat to separate the backbone from the carcass. Using a heavy knife or cleaver, cut the breast, bones and all, in half widthwise. Then cut each half in half along the keel bone so that you have four equal pieces of breast on the bone.

Save the backbone and wings and any other bone and cartilage for stock. You could also roast them and add them to the stew; or you could roast them and make stock to fortify the cooking liquid. But for this stew I'm not using the carcass or the bones. *Maman* wouldn't have had time to roast them separately or to make a stock.

Chop the skin and fat to render it. The finer you do this, the more efficiently the fat will render. Render it on the stove top, starting it with a little water, or simply put it in a 200°F oven. My mother did it on the stove top. Strain the fat and reserve the cracklings for topping a salad.

Put the goose pieces in a container that will allow all of them to fit in one tight layer.

Freshly ground pepper, plenty of it
8 to 10 sprigs thyme
2 bay leaves
4 or 5 cloves garlic
1 medium onion, thinly sliced
2 carrots, peeled and sliced
2 stalks celery, sliced
1 bottle Riesling

Cover the goose pieces with freshly ground pepper, using a fine setting and making twenty or thirty grinds. I like a lot of pepper. Do not salt the goose—I think it pickles the meat in a marinade and affects the texture. There will be time for seasoning it in the stew.

Top the pieces with plenty of fresh thyme. (This is not what my mother did, by the way. We didn't *have* fresh thyme in Alsace—it grew in the south, not where we lived, so we only used dried thyme. But I use it now because, happily, fresh thyme is abundant today.) Add the two bay leaves and four or five cloves of garlic. Sprinkle the sliced onion over the pieces, then add the sliced carrots and sliced stalks of celery. Drizzle half of the bottle of Riesling all over the goose. (The last time I made this, I asked my brother Philippe for an inexpensive one, which is what you should use—but he gave me a grand cru; it was all we had. It would have do!) Cover the container and refrigerate it overnight.

Rendered goose fat as needed
Kosher salt as needed

When you're ready to cook your goose, remove it from the marinade. Strain the marinade, reserving both the liquid and the vegetables, in separate containers. Bring the liquid to a simmer in a small pan, then strain it through a fine mesh strainer. The blood leached out in the marinade will coagulate—you want to strain this out along with any herbs and seasonings.

Next, brown the meat. Heat a large sauté pan over medium-high heat, then coat the bottom with a generous layer of the rendered goose fat. When the fat ripples, add the pieces of goose in one layer, giving them plenty of room, so that they don't crowd each other and steam. You'll likely need to brown them in two batches. This browning adds flavor and color, and it also sets the protein, so that it won't coagulate in the stew and rise as a grayish mat. Salt the goose pieces now as you're browning them. Cook them until they're nicely browned. Put the first batch of pieces in a Dutch oven or large pot and brown the remaining pieces in more goose fat as needed.

When all the goose pieces are browned and in the Dutch oven, add the vegetables to the sauté pan and brown these, adding more goose fat as necessary. Salt them. (You can do this in a separate pan while you're cooking the goose if you want to save time.) Once they're browned, add the vegetables to the Dutch oven that holds the goose pieces. The browned meat and the browned vegetables will give the sauce a rich color. Pour the remaining wine into the Dutch oven, along with the strained marinade and enough water just to cover the goose. Add another four-finger pinch of salt and bring it all to a simmer. Cover the pot and lower the heat so that the liquid just simmers, or put the pot in a 300°F oven until the goose is tender, two to three hours. The water and the wine will dissolve the tough connective tissue—the tough meat, the bones, the cartilage—of the goose to give you a rich sauce. The meat will flavor the sauce but without cooking for so long that the water takes out all the flavor, as it will in a stock. The browning of the meat and vegetables will add flavor, sweetness, and color to the sauce.

1 cup cold coffee
Flour as needed (about ½ cup)

When the goose is almost done, put the cold coffee in a pot or a bowl. Whisk in enough flour so that the coffee is very thick but pourable, twice as thick as cream. Sprinkle the flour in gradually while whisking so that it doesn't clump. This is how my mother made a slurry, Chinese-style! She'd never have bothered to prepare a traditional roux. She'd just carefully whisk the flour in as she sprinkled it over the coffee so it didn't lump up and then she'd immediately stir it into the hot cooking liquid.

With the uncovered Dutch oven containing the goose on the stove and simmering gently, taste the braising liquid and adjust the seasoning as needed. Slowly add the coffee slurry, stirring, until the sauce has thickened. It should be appealingly rich—not thick like a paste, just a lovely sauce consistency.

Serve one piece of goose per person, with braised red cabbage, mashed potatoes or spaetzle, and a salad with a sharp vinaigrette, topped with the goose cracklings.

SERVES 10

My dad, Georges, loved to cook and had the patience
to make elaborate meals on Sundays while the rest
of us were in church. My mom, Jeanine, did all the
cooking of lunches and dinners for the family and for
all the employees and guests of their coal business.

2.

HUSTLE

I HATED SCHOOL. BY THE TIME I WAS A TEENAGER, MY parents had enrolled me in an engineering program so that I'd be prepared to enter the wonderful world of coal. The oldest son was expected to go into the family business, but I had no interest in coal. I hated coal. It was filthy. My father worked his butt off, and I could see what a grind it was, especially the never-ending task of chasing down the people who owed them money.

What I loved was putting on parties. When I was eight, my younger brothers and older sister started asking me to put on their birthday parties. I did, and I loved it. When my sister became a teenager, she asked me to create parties for her every weekend. So every Saturday night I set up parties in our cellar, painting the walls, creating the lighting, lining up the music I would play. I loved to entertain. I loved having lots of people around. That was when I was happiest. Actually, I didn't paint the walls at age eight (that would come later, as my entertaining became more elaborate), but even at a young age I recognized the importance of lighting. I'd put all the table lamps on the floor, which would be much better for us kids. My mom was always baking cookies and tarts, and I would serve these. But parties weren't about food, they were about fun. I wasn't into cooking then, and so I never connected it with entertaining.

School? I had so little desire for formal learning that I didn't do anything, or I did as little as possible, until the school kicked me out. I was expelled. My parents were furious. My father didn't speak to me for weeks. I may well have been diagnosed with ADD, if that had been something kids got tested for in those days. But back then I was just considered a good-for-nothing screw-up. Which was why my father wouldn't talk to me for months.

But when my sixteenth birthday came around, March 16, 1973, my father felt guilty about not talking to me. His eldest son was inevitably becoming a man, and he decided to celebrate my birthday with a grand dinner. Just me, my mother, and him. He had a client in the next village, about a forty-five-minute drive away. We almost never went out to restaurants at all. *Maman* always cooked. If we did go out, it was a really big occasion.

In this town, where my father regularly went on business, was a restaurant called Auberge de l'Ill. It was recognized as the best in the area and long ago had earned three Michelin stars, the highest and most exclusive rating in the country, and it had maintained that status. Auberge was the *only* Michelin three-star in that part of France, and it was owned and run by chef Paul Haeberlin.

My father felt it was time to begin talking to me, and so he, my mother, and I celebrated my sixteenth birthday with a dinner at Auberge.

I have always loved food, loved to eat. And my mother was a great cook, as I've said. My childhood was filled with beautiful scents from the kitchen, stews and roasts, the wonderful rotting smells of fermenting cabbage in our cellar, soft smelly cheeses, and sweet buttery tarts baking in the afternoon.

And my mom's cousin Gaston ran a small brasserie in Otswald, the next village over from ours in the other direction. It served traditional Alsatian fare—potato salad with knockwurst, onion tarts, tartes flambées. We'd sometimes go there, though not often, because my mother didn't think Gaston could cook. And she was right. It was just him and a couple guys in back, drinking as much as they were cooking; they did a lot of parties on the weekends. But *Maman* shook her head—Gaston had never learned proper techniques. They did a good business hosting weddings and parties on the weekends, and sometimes I'd go there to help out. I didn't recognize it at the time, but the kitchen was a disaster. I just knew I didn't like it there. This was pretty much my only notion of what a restaurant was, whereas frankly, our kitchen was busier and better than Gaston's.

All of which is to say that all I knew of the food world was Gaston's brasserie and my own kitchen, so that *nothing* could have prepared me for Auberge de l'Ill. Forty-five years later, that meal in 1973 remains one of the most enduring memories of my life.

The menu listed six dishes the restaurant was famous for, so I chose from those. I started with the foie gras. My mother always made several pounds of foie gras at Christmastime, and I loved it. But I'd never had it wrapped around a truffle, surrounded by a sweet-acidic gelée and a delicate crust. Oh. My. God. I would eventually learn that Haeberlin was renowned for his foie gras, that preparing it was the highlight of his day—it was his way of relaxing and unwinding every afternoon. He was a master of foie gras. I only knew that I was seeing and tasting something extraordinary for the first time.

My second course—and I remember each dish as clearly now as if I were back there—was *mousseline de grenouilles,* frogs' legs with Riesling and watercress. For my entrée I chose a medallion of venison, from a deer local hunters had brought to the chef, served with apples and cranberries; it came with the first classical reduction sauce I'd tasted. Amazing. And for dessert I ordered another house specialty, a poached peach with pistachio ice cream. The chef preserved a good supply of local peaches every summer to serve all year long; jarred in a light syrup for months, they were more intensely flavored than when they'd been fresh.

There weren't words for my astonishment. I hadn't known that food could be this way, could have such an impact.

When Chef Haeberlin came to the table, my father said to him, "This guy's good for nothing," tilting his head at me. He wasn't kidding—he really meant it. "Do you need anyone to wash dishes or peel potatoes?" he asked with a laugh, as a joke. But the chef said, "Actually, I'm looking for an apprentice."

What my father didn't know, what the chef didn't know, what even *I* didn't know or have words for but sensed deep down was this: I *belonged* here. I knew it that night, I knew it without knowing it. The intensity and finesse of the food. The beauty of the room. The choreography of the captain and the waiters and the chef at our table. The luxury of it all. It was like a movie set, like sitting inside the greatest movie ever. This was where I belonged—I knew it. I thought, *"This is going to be my life."*

*

MY FATHER CALLED THE CHEF the next morning, and I was able to spend a day in the kitchen. I ran around all day, asking what I could do. Kissing up to everybody. I *hustled*. I had one day to show Monsieur Paul who I was. I ran *everywhere*.

Monsieur Paul said to me, "You sure have a lot of energy." I thought, "Yes, I do, because I need this! I need to be here."

I loved the kitchen, I loved the action. I didn't want the day to end.

But end it did, and I was back in the house, and . . . *nothing*. A week went by, and then another. Then the month of April. I felt horrible. They didn't *like* me. The month of May passed. Not a word from Monsieur Paul. Another month passed. My father grew angry. "You've failed at this, too," he grumbled at me. I felt humiliated. Nevertheless, by the end of June, I was over the defeat. I was still happy. This is how I was then and still am—if I suffer a defeat, I sleep it off and I move forward. Don't look back.

And look at what I did have. I had a bed. I had girls to flirt with! My mother was a great cook. All the cakes and tarts I could eat—my favorite was the *kougelhopf*, every

Sunday morning, when the bakeries were closed. She also made a great pound cake—known as *quatre quart* in French—only she put 50 percent more butter in, so it was very rich. She made an amazing *tarte au fromage blanc,* white cheese with lemon zest and sugar and eggs, a lot like a cheesecake but much more elegant and so delicious, and a Mirabelle tart, using little French plums. What more does a sixteen-year-old need? I knew that something would work out. I wanted clean, I wanted away from coal, away from home. I knew that something would come along. And so it did.

Bastille Day, July 14, occasions such a big celebration in France that you go out the night before with your friends and party till dawn. This was exactly what I was looking forward to when, at five o'clock on July 13, my father came to me and said that Monsieur Paul had called. I was to begin work the following day at eight in the morning.

I said, "No way—I'm going out with my friends tonight. Can I start on the fifteenth?" I didn't know how restaurants worked—that in restaurants, while others are enjoying the holidays with their families, the cooks are working. Of course, I was excited to have heard from the restaurant, but I didn't want to let my friends down.

My father said, "You can go out tonight. And tomorrow morning, I'm waking you at six and dropping you off at the restaurant at eight."

I said, "Okay."

And that was when my life began.

3.

START IN PASTRY

WHEN I ARRIVED IN THE KITCHEN OF AUBERGE DE L'ILL on Bastille Day, the first thing I saw was that the stoves were heated by coal. Oh, I knew coal. I knew all the different kinds of coal and how they burned. I knew what a mess coal was. I hated coal. I was trying to get away from coal. And again I was surrounded by it.

Fortunately, it was the dishwashers' job to light the fires in the stoves every morning. Still, coal dust was always in the air, reminding me about where I came from and what I strove to put behind me.

My first position was in pastry, as was true for every starting apprentice, and I had little clue as to how lucky I was to begin there. I wasn't passionate about cooking at the time; I wanted to be where the action was, and the action was in the hot kitchen. I'd always cooked with my mother and grandmother, was always tasting. I loved to eat, and I had a good palate. By cooking with my mother, I had developed a sense for seasoning. But at home, cooking was just a way to help out in a busy house and a kitchen that fed dozens of people every day. Me, I mainly loved to eat.

So I wasn't born with an innate passion for cooking. What I did have a passion for was organizing. And in a kitchen, organizing is as important a skill as knowing how to handle a knife.

Monsieur Paul, I learned, started every apprentice in pastry for a reason. Pastry is all about precision. We measured everything on a scale to the gram. And to this day, that's how I still do all my recipes, everything to the gram. This makes them consistent no matter who is in the kitchen that day. Monsieur Paul knew that once you learn precision, the rest will follow. But if you begin learning speed or get thrown into cooking right away, developing the habit of precision is much more difficult, like acquiring a second language.

Learn precision first, and the rest will follow.

*

MY PARENTS MIGHT HAVE BEEN disappointed that I wasn't learning the family business, but at least I was working at something. I was no longer a good-for-nothing; nevertheless, they were still worried. Every time they saw the chef, they'd ask, "How's he doing? Is he going to make it?" My father figured that since I'd screwed up everything else I'd tried—I got into some kind of trouble on pretty much a daily basis—I'd screw this up, too. Every week he expected me to tell him I'd been fired.

Which is kind of humiliating when I think about it, because back then, being a cook was not respected. Taking a job in a kitchen was not something you bragged about. It was a vocation you did because you couldn't do anything better. Most of my friends were still in school. They would go on to study medicine and engineering and move into white-collar professions. No one was a cook. And so at first I told no one about what I was doing.

One of my parents would drop me off on Tuesday morning, and they would pick me up Sunday after lunch, the last service of the week. During the week, I lived in a room above the restaurant with one of the other two apprentices. There was usually a first-year, a second-year, and a third-year apprentice. This work replaced school. It's hard to imagine kids leaving school at sixteen today. But times were different in the early 1970s. We would work six days a week, including going to classes at nine a.m. one day a week, every Friday; these taught us kitchen principles and how to run a restaurant. We had to be back at the restaurant by six for service.

This was our life. You don't have much of a social life when you work in a kitchen and live above it; even so, we managed to have good times when we could. I would soon start dating Monsieur Paul's daughter. She was younger than I was, and we kept it a secret. Outside work, I went out with the other apprentices. We were given a small sum for sundries, but we mainly worked for room and board and the hope of an apprentice's certificate, which would guarantee us a job. None of us had a car, so we'd sneak away to the bar across the street, although we couldn't stay out late because we lived at the restaurant and the creaking steps would announce our arrival.

For the most part, it was work from morning until the kitchen was cleaned after the dinner service. We'd rise at eight in the morning, and by eight-thirty all the cooks were in the kitchen. Monsieur Paul's mother made us all coffee each morning and served us pastries, *viennoiseries*. Then we would get to work. And this was my life for the first year. Tuesday through Sunday at the restaurant, learning to be a cook. Sunday evening and Monday at home. My other friends would have gone out on Friday and Saturday nights and need to be in on Sunday night, which was really my only night off, my Saturday night. They had to be in school the next day, so I rarely went out with them. I caught up with them by phone, watched TV. My parents were still happy that I hadn't been fired, and I was, too. I'd found that I was good in the kitchen, and I was glad to be good at something. I became ensconced in the solitary life of a cook.

If you see me in my restaurants, you'll notice that I'm always bouncing around from one guest to the next, to a server, to a cook, to one of my directors, or to my younger brother Philippe, long a member of the team; I'm always talking business, chatting with customers. I am outwardly gregarious, and usually happy, but I am by nature an introvert. I need solitude. And as a young cook, I had this solitary nature as well.

Often my first job of the day was to get the milk. Today, plastic milk crates are delivered to the restaurant by truck. But at Auberge, we walked to a farmhouse down the road, to the farmer who sold us milk. We carried it back in big metal milk cans that were heavy as hell. Next we'd go to the chicken farmer and pick up the birds. And the eggs.

This experience was critical to me as an apprentice. I saw how the animals were raised, what they were fed. I learned about the chickens and the egg cycle. If you are an aspiring chef, you should work on a farm if you get the opportunity. You should know that eggs don't just come in a carton. It takes about seven days for a chicken to produce an egg, from ovulation to laying. When you understand that, you recognize that when you carelessly drop an egg on the floor, you don't just have a mess to clean up. You recognize that it will take seven days to get that egg back, and maybe next time you'll take more care with the eggs.

My first job in pastry was to make the ice cream bases, starting with vanilla. We measured yolks to the gram. I would learn to make pistachio ice cream, the same dish that had ended the meal that changed my life, and I poached the preserved peaches.

It wasn't a big department—just right for learning. We had an executive pastry chef, one *chef de partie* (station chef), two *commis* (prep cooks), and one apprentice, me.

Soon I moved on to sorbets, learning one thing at a time. I was fascinated by the cherry sorbet. I stemmed and pitted the cherries. Then the cherries were turned into juice. I was instructed to put the pits, the *noyaux,* in a bag, and to crack them with a hammer. The pits of many stone fruits release a heady, bitter-almond flavor, so I would soak the *noyaux* in the cherry juice for twelve hours. It made the cherry flavor deeper and more complex than if you skipped this step and threw the pits out.

I learned the whole range of French patisserie in that one kitchen, the way most cooks did. I made praline parfaits, *nougatine,* chocolate cake, crème brûlée, and cookies such as the *langues de chat,* cat's tongues; I learned how to make a laminated dough, puff pastry, every manner of tart and petit four.

One of Monsieur Paul's desserts was a peach poached in simple syrup, served with the pit. That was important—the pit has so much flavor. We served this peach with a sabayon. This is where I learned how to make a sabayon. It was so good and so simple, I still remember it and even make it today. Here it is: twelve yolks, 200 grams of sugar, a bottle of champagne. You whip it over high heat until it comes to a boil, and that's it. Amazingly, it never curdles—it turns into a thick, rich sauce.

This recognition of the flavor of pits and seeds may be coming back. On a trip to Paris recently, we were served a pre-dessert bite of a single peeled apple seed. I thought, "What is this, are you kidding me?" Then I ate it. It was one of the most flavorful things I've ever tasted.

We prepared a whole range of traditional desserts, petit fours, and *mignardises*. Lemon and strawberry tarts, chocolate cake, and chocolate ganache. I learned how to make puff pastry. But mainly what I learned was precision. We weighed everything. This was important, because back then you didn't weigh anything unless you had to. After I left pastry, I would rarely use a scale.

Once service began, the tickets arrived furiously, and I learned how to read-order-fire dishes—that is, understand what orders were coming in and which dishes needed to be prepared when. And I would help plate the desserts, the designs of which had to be perfectly executed.

I loved it all.

*

AFTER SEVERAL MONTHS, I'd had enough of ice creams and cakes and soufflés and parfaits. I wanted to *cook*. I wanted to be in the hot kitchen, coal and all. I wanted to be where the action was. I went to the chef de cuisine, second-in-command in the kitchen, and said, "I came here to cook, not to do pastry." But Monsieur Paul—he was always "Monsieur Paul," never "Chef"—kept me in pastry for six months, as he did all the apprentices. The time I spent there was more valuable than I could have foreseen. And what it taught me, though I didn't recognize it then, was patience. When you are young and ambitious, you want to move quickly, before you are ready. Growth takes time; you must learn patience. Learn one skill, become better at it by repeating it over and over, slowly working toward perfecting it before moving on. There is no substitute for time spent running in place, building your muscles and your skills.

*

WHEN I MOVED OUT OF PASTRY, a new apprentice took my place. This was how the kitchen worked, how it replenished itself.

I moved to the garde-manger station, cold food preparations. First I learned Monsieur Paul's vinaigrettes. They were extraordinary. One was a kind of rémoulade with chopped egg, capers, and cornichons, but its salt component was caviar. It was *half* caviar. I hesitate to call it a caviar vinaigrette, yet that's what it was. And we used it only for the freshly smoked sturgeon, the fish that *gives* us the caviar, of course.

I learned a traditional grainy mustard vinaigrette that

used sunflower oil, the neutral oil of the region. We emulsified it in a blender. Monsieur Paul taught me to add a couple of tablespoons of warm water to it, to lighten it and help make the emulsion stronger. And we did an amazing lobster vinaigrette, more like a mayonnaise, an orange mayonnaise, because we used the fat that solidified on top of the lobster stock. We served this on a terrine of lobster and langoustine.

Once I'd learned the vinaigrettes and the salads and the other cold dishes, I moved on to fish. Monsieur Paul was very smart the way he trained us. We weren't all over the kitchen. We learned one thing at a time. When we had mastered it, mastered it at the level of a three-star Michelin restaurant, we moved on. First stocks, then sauces; how to butcher flat fish and round fish, then how to cook them, then their sauces; meat butchery, from small birds to larger animals, and so on.

I learned to butcher fish, fileting every salmon, yellow pike, and other freshwater fish of the region. A truck from the south arrived once a week so we could sometimes serve saltwater fish, John Dory and turbot. But mainly, being so far inland, we prepared river fish. Carp, crayfish, frogs' legs, and eel.

The eel dish was a delicious preparation, but also my daily nemesis. The eels came in alive, and I had to hang them on butcher hooks. I cut a slit around their necks; then, gripping the skin with a kitchen towel, I yanked the skin off. The skin does not come off easily, and the live eels whipped and writhed and wrapped themselves around my arm. It was like living in a nightmare. After I got the skin off, they would bleed out. It's a pretty shocking experience

for a sixteen- or seventeen-year-old. They were still writh-
ing when they went into the cooking pot.

But they were tasty. Monsieur Paul created a matelote—
fish fumet, an Alsatian pinot noir, mushrooms, pearl
onions, and lardons. This liquid reduced as it cooked,
intensifying in flavor. We finished it with a fresh splash of
red wine and mounted it with butter. Monsieur Paul served
it with spaetzle, the long kind, made by spreading the batter on a board and using a long knife to cut the noodles
straight into boiling water. (This was customary in the
Haut-Rhin, the high part of the valley; in the Bas-Rhin,
the Lower Rhine, people made them the way my mother
did, by dropping the spaetzle off a spoon.)

We cooked the salmon within a mousseline. We used
the pike for the mousseline, passing it through a sieve
because it's such a bony fish. We used the same mousse
for the frogs' legs, the mousseline I'd had on my first visit
to Auberge and had loved. The legs were cooked, and the
bones were removed. Then we made a kind of ragout from
them, and we filled the center of the mousseline with this;
after baking the mousseline, we turned it out onto the
plate. When you broke into the mousseline, the frogs' leg
ragout spilled out. It was so good.

Monsieur Paul often had *truite au bleu* on the menu,
a dish where the fish is dipped in vinegar. The acid reacts
with the skin and turns it blue. It's imperative to work
with not just the freshest trout available but fish that are
still alive when service begins. So when the order was
called, I'd put down two pots, one with butter, another
with vinegar. I had already made a batch of mirepoix
before service—shallots, carrots, thyme, rosemary, a cou-

ple cloves of garlic—and I would get that into the butter to sweat it for the court bouillon. Then I'd run outside to fetch the trout, in the snow if it was winter. They swam in a small basin behind the restaurant. I'd catch one in a net, and I'd knock it on the head with a wooden spatula. Hard, hard enough to stun it but not so hard that I'd damage the head. I'd run it into the kitchen, open it up, and gut it. I had to get all the blood out, which I did by dragging my finger along the inside of the spine. There's a lot of blood in a trout, and it's nearly black. Then I'd roll it in Melfor vinegar—the vinegar of the region—so that it was completely covered in acid, and it would turn bright, bright blue, the slime from the fish reacting with the vinegar. I'd add the mirepoix to the vinegar and stock to finish the court bouillon.

But I couldn't just toss the trout in the pot and let it cook, as I did with every other meat or fish. I had to stand there holding it upright, in the position in which it was accustomed to swimming, until it began to curl and the flesh firmed up. Only after that could I leave it to prepare other dishes whose orders were coming in, allowing it to poach for eight minutes. When it was done, I brought it to the pass, the junction in the kitchen where dishes are inspected before being carried into the dining area. Monsieur Paul put it in a towel and carried it in a towel to the table, still steaming. While he was doing that, I made the *beurre fondue,* half butter and half strained poaching liquid, with lots and lots of herbs. Dill, parsley, chervil chive, tarragon—almost as much herbs as butter. Timing was critical. When the trout went to the table to be filleted tableside, the *beurre fondue,* along with the parsley potatoes and spinach that went with the dish, had better be at the pass or I'd be in the shit. All that for one dish, *truite au bleu*. While other orders poured in.

This was when I saw that I had to be super-organized, and that we all had to work as a team. And I found that I liked this, being part of a team.

*

NEXT IT WAS ON TO the meat station; as with fish, the apprentices began with butchery. The first task was breaking down the birds. Today all the birds arrive at the restaurant plucked and in a bag, but at Auberge all the birds came still warm and feathered and it was my job to pluck them. Most birds today are scalded first to make taking out their feathers easier. But Monsieur Paul didn't like the texture of the skin of scalded birds, so I had to pluck them dry. It was hard work. Nevertheless, every day I tried to work faster and more efficiently. I liked this work; I knew I was good at it. My body naturally had the energy for twelve- to fifteen-hour days, hustling all the time, and this contributed to my motivation to get better.

All the birds—the partridges, the woodcocks—had to hang. You don't see these birds on menus anymore, sadly. The ducks hung for six days. It was especially important to hang the pheasants—*faisans* in French. Pheasant meat is very mild and needs to begin rotting to develop flavor. Time spent hanging is so important that we turned the noun into a verb, *faisander*.

I learned the muscle structure of the birds and how to prepare them for cooking. Then I learned the muscles and bone structure of venison, of lamb.

When I finally made it to the stoves, I remembered how much I hated coal. So much soot. It gets in your mouth. You can feel it coating your teeth. I can't imagine those earlier eminent chefs—like Fernand Point, chef-owner of the famed La Pyramide and the teacher of Bocuse, the Troisgros brothers, and so many other greats—cooking their whole life with coal. Even with the hoods you could taste it. It was messing up my palate. The dishwashers were charged with feeding the fires, but I was glad when, the second year I was there, around 1975, we moved to gas.

I loved the cleanliness of the kitchen, loved working as part of a team, and I loved the basics of cooking. Once I realized that I had to learn patience and work my way through pastry before moving forward, taking each discipline step by step, I loved everything about cooking and life in the kitchen.

It's remarkable when I pause and look at where we are now and what I learned then—nearly fifty years ago, hard to believe. The kitchen and our food are both so different today. So, is what I learned back then still relevant? Of course it is. As I said, I still make the sabayon the same way; but, more to the point, I still season the same way. The basics don't change.

What has changed, though, are the flavors and composition of our dishes. Back then, every dish, whether fish or meat, had its own sauce. Beef would require a beef stock, squab its own squab sauce. That's not so today—we tend to mix flavors, serving turbot with a beef *jus*, for instance, or a tea infusion or a vinaigrette or a curry. Today we get inspired by dishes from Mexico, from Africa, from Malaysia—and we mix flavors. Of course, we still braise short ribs in the traditional way—and I love them. But I haven't used a classical brown veal stock since the 1980s. Back then, just about everything was finished with butter or cream. That's not what we want anymore.

But back then there was also much less waste. Today, though I serve a lot of fish at my restaurant, we almost never make a fish fumet. And if we did, it would be in a pressure cooker! This means we throw away a lot of bones simply because our clientele won't order enough fish soup to make it worthwhile. Back then, you would never throw away a fish head. And when you pluck a chicken yourself, you're going to make sure you use everything except the beak. But forward we move.

As I've said, the basics don't change, and my basics, fortunately, began in pastry, with the importance of weighing ingredients. And, of course, it helped that I was learning the basics at a Michelin three-star, France's highest level.

Me with Monsieur Paul Bocuse, c. 1970.

4.

BEGIN IN THE BEST KITCHEN YOU CAN, THEN RAISE THE BAR

AFTER TWO YEARS WITH MONSIEUR PAUL, IT WAS TIME for my apprentice exam.

In France when I grew up, an apprenticeship was an actual, accredited program, with a test and a certificate of completion at the end, if you passed. It was called *le certificat d'aptitude professionnelle*, or CAP, and while it still exists in some form, when I was coming up it was the only way to train. You couldn't get a job in a kitchen without your CAP. You apprenticed in a restaurant for two years: five days a week in the kitchen, one day a week in a classroom, learning numbers and food costs and the whys of cooking, how butter becomes a Hollandaise and why an emulsion works, why a stock is clear and not cloudy, how to clarify a consommé. But in the end it all came down to the one test comprising a written exam and a cooking practical. Was I nervous. Monsieur Paul told me, "If you fail, you can't come back."

I said, "Okay." Then I hardly slept at all the night before the test.

For the cooking practical, we had the possibility of

drawing one of twelve menus. We didn't know what we were going to get until we were in the kitchen and we drew the slip of paper from a bowl. We weren't allowed to use books or notes. We had to prepare the three-course menu we drew using only memory and knowledge of technique. It was a lot like *Iron Chef*!

The recipes were from a small textbook we used that contained about seventy recipes. Some were basic, others were elaborate, and many were traditional to Alsace— sauerkraut dishes, onion tarts, and the *baeckeoffe*, which I still love. This is a dish from my childhood, a terrine lay-ered with various meats and root vegetables. The name translates to "baker's oven," because it was traditionally a Jewish casserole that would be made for the Sabbath, when Jews were forbidden to cook; everyone in the com-munity would take their casseroles to the local baker, who would put the dishes in the oven after the bread was done, so that a meal would be ready by the afternoon.

In Monsieur Paul's kitchen, one of my jobs was to cook the family meal, which is to say the staff meal, once a week. Most days there were two women who cooked the family meal, but one day a week Monsieur Paul had the apprentice cook the family meal.

Cooking the staff meal was how I practiced for my apprentice exam. The staff loved it because dishes such as lamb *printanière* were on the test, a rack of lamb roasted and served with spring vegetables. Not a bad family meal! That was how I learned to tell when a rack of lamb was done by touch, by squeezing it—from repetition while cooking for the staff. You can't use a thermometer during the test; you can't poke anything into the meat to see if it's cold or hot in the center. You learn by doing, by cooking and touching and paying attention each time.

Here was another reason I was lucky to have started in a three-star kitchen: I got to practice each of the twelve dishes for six months before the test.

The family meal also teaches the importance of timing and planning. If you're roasting chickens for seventy staff, that's twenty chickens or so. A chicken takes an hour in the oven, but if you put twenty birds in the oven, they're going to take longer, an hour and fifteen, an hour and a half; the oven has only so much heat to put into the cold food. The first time I made roast chicken for the staff, I pulled the chickens in time to allow them to rest and then to be carved. But Monsieur Paul saw the chickens, cut into one, and it was bloody. He was furious. We didn't have any time to waste in the kitchen, with a very small gap in which to serve seventy people and allow them to eat without rushing. I had to cut all the chickens into pieces and roast them again. It was horrible, and I was ashamed. I never forgot this lesson—that there are many factors affecting what you are cooking, and that you have to be aware of them all.

*

BEFORE THE APPRENTICES could take the cooking practical, we had to take a written test first, twenty questions about all the things we learned in class. There was no point in cooking if you couldn't pass that. That part was easy, even for me, with my hatred of school and written work. Because I liked to cook, learning why an emulsion forms or defining *remouillage,* the second veal stock, was fun.

So the written test, short answers and definitions, was simple. It was the cooking practical that we were all anxious about. As I've mentioned, I couldn't sleep before the day of the test, I was so nervous. In my mind, I kept hearing Monsieur Paul say, "If you fail, you can't come back." Oh my God.

There were twelve of us, between Auberge and the nearby restaurant kitchens. Six or seven chefs would be judging us. Monsieur Paul was one of them, but he couldn't evaluate me because I worked for him. The judges loved the day of the test. It began at eight, and they drank wine all day, while we cooked. We had six hours to complete the entire menu—stocks and all.

We were evaluated first on our hygiene. Were our fingernails clean, were our uniforms spotless, did we have crisp creases in our jackets? This was easy for me. Ever since I was a boy, I had loved being precise in my appearance, loved stacking perfectly folded shirts on my shelves. My hair was short by then—I no longer looked like a girl from behind! (It was the early seventies, and as a teenager I'd grown my hair quite long. That didn't fly in Monsieur Paul's kitchen.) I was always very clean, though. Nothing on my jacket, no scraps of food on my shoes.

Shoes are important. Look around in kitchens. Even sometimes at Jean-Georges, cooks walk around with a week's worth of *mise en place* on their shoes. Parsley, dried chicken stock, scraps of meat, flecks of minced shallot. You can learn a lot about a cook by looking at their shoes. Many journalists have written that I wear Prada loafers in the kitchen. It's true. Sometimes I do. Certainly, I appreciate excellent shoes. But they also remind me of the cook I always strive to be, someone who works so clean that he can wear the finest shoes in the kitchen. This means something to me.

It *all* means something, from your hair to your fingernails to your shoes. Pay attention to how you look. It is not a reflection of you or your work, it is an *extension* of it, it *is* you.

Of course, what you wear and how you look is the easy part. The cooking and the delivering of perfectly prepared food on time—that's the hard part.

So on the night before the test, I couldn't sleep. I stayed in bed until six and was in the kitchen by seven-thirty. Once all the apprentices had arrived, we drew our menus. My dream was to get the foie gras terrine, because this was easy and delicious and I'd learned how to make it from Monsieur Paul, whose foie gras was the best in the land. Because during the exam there would be no time to marinate it, as he did, you had to be aggressive with the seasoning, but that was the only adjustment. Clean the goose liver well—always goose, in Alsace, never duck—removing all the veins; season it with salt and white pepper, some wine; pack it in a terrine mold and cook it in a water bath; then chill it, unmold it, and slice it; serve it with gelée and toasted brioche—easy.

The rack of lamb was my favorite, though cooking it and judging its doneness was tricky, and the presentation was painstaking. You had to hit the temperature just right relative to when you intended to slice and serve it. This was back in the days of tableside service, when large cuts of meat were presented at the table, then sliced and served. Roasted lamb *printanière* was not simply sautéing two chops in a pan. These were seven-rib racks, which we had to butcher, trim, and French, then serve, crossing the ribs and placing doilies on the ends.

My wish for dessert was to draw the Alsatian apple tart, one of my favorites to make and to eat. In this version of the apple tart, apples and sugar are cooked until caramelized, then laid down in a blind-baked *pâte brisée*. Vanilla custard is poured into the shell so that the apples are almost covered, just enough custard so that the edges of the apple stick out and brown as the custard cooks.

No one wanted to draw the *blanquette de veau*, which would take every minute of our allotted time, or the very difficult *merlan frit en colère*. *Merlan* is whiting, a fish common in the North Atlantic. For this dish you had to clean four fish and remove each one's gills. You then had to curl each fish into a circle, catching the tail in the cut where the gills had been. The fish were then floured and deep-fried. A lot of work at the last minute, and a real pain to keep each one of them in the proper shape.

We all drew, and I was ecstatic to pick the lamb *printanière* and the Alsatian apple tart. Alas, another of my colleagues drew the foie gras terrine. Instead, I drew the soup, *cultivateur*, essentially a chicken vegetable soup, which is not difficult, but you start with nothing, so I would need to make the stock first thing. All the vegetables must be precisely cut and perfectly cooked upon serving.

Of course, we would be graded on everything, including waste. We first had to write out our lists—all the food we would need, and then a prep list and a time line—and we would be graded on these, too. Then we gathered everything we needed to complete our recipes, the exact amounts for everything. Take too much, so that you must return what you don't need, or take too little, so that you need to go back for more, and you lose points. If you forgot to put peas on your list, you could still go back and get them, but you'd be penalized.

The chefs left their glasses of Riesling to walk the kitchen, pads in hand, as we cooked. They noted how we used our knives, how clean our stations were. How well we peeled our vegetables. Were we keeping waste to a minimum? The meats didn't come in trimmed and ready to cook—the chefs wanted to grade us on our butchering skills. We had to use all our trim or we'd lose points. We had to cut our vegetables using every bit of them—if there was too much waste, if we left too much onion on the core, points would come off. Waste was a big deal back then. If we were making a stock, they would evaluate its clarity. It must be clear—*limpide,* in French. If they saw that you'd let your stock come to a boil, clouding it, more points would be taken off.

I was very organized. I began my chicken stock first. Then I butchered the lamb, so that I could use the trimmings for a *jus.* This, too, had to be *limpide.* I'd pass it through a chinois, and it would be finished with *beurre monté.* The chefs, I thought as I worked, they're watching me. They're judging us, getting tipsy.

My root vegetables—carrots, turnips, potato—had to be tournéed. This cut, a seven-sided football shape, takes some practice. The judges would actually count to make sure each one had seven sides. All my vegetables for the *printanière* had to be glazed. All had different cooking times, so each would have to be cooked in its own copper pot. My method for glazing root vegetables was to bring water about three-quarters of the way up the vegetables, add a knob of butter, and cover the pot with a parchment lid, which would allow just the right amount of evaporation. Once the water was gone, the vegetables would be perfectly cooked, and they could be finished with butter. The green vegetables—peas, favas, haricots verts—would be glazed separately, of course.

The service itself was easy if you started off organized and had your timing planned out. I decided to serve my soup in a tureen, so that would be simple to have ready when it was my turn to present. And my tart would be cooked in advance and served whole. It was only the presentation of the lamb, followed by its carving and the serving of the vegetables, that could be tricky.

My soup was perfect, as was the tart, with no bubbles in the perfectly creamy custard. I nailed the temperature of my lamb. I lost points only for some of my green vegetables, which the judges found too al dente. But I *passed*.

All except one of us passed, in fact, the one who had the *merlans frit en colère*. The whiting was to be fried in the shape of a ring, served with parsley potatoes and tartar sauce. He hadn't prepared the fish properly, and so they came apart in the oil. He had four fish, and not one of them held their shape. And he was a mess, flour everywhere; I was glad I hadn't drawn that dish, because that was a tough one. But you could do it if you worked clean and organized.

I returned to my restaurant that afternoon. Everyone asked, "Did you pass, did you pass?" I said, "Yes!" And they all gave me a hard time, razzing me and saying it was only because Monsieur Paul had been one of the judges. But they popped a bottle of champagne, and we drank. I'd earned my certificate.

I still have it.

*

IRONICALLY, IN THE END, I didn't need it. I never used it. Though I didn't realize it at the time, I was already part of the mafia, the chef mafia. There were relatively few Michelin three-star chefs in France, and so, naturally, they formed a kind of exclusive group—a mafia. Since I was doing so well in Monsieur Paul's three-star kitchen, I could go to virtually any other three-star kitchen that was hiring. What would have been difficult for me, if not impossible, would have been to go "down" to a two- or one-star restaurant. I didn't set out to do this, but the lesson for me is to work in the very best kitchen you can at the outset and then never go back. Always keep raising the bar for yourself.

ON THE ROAD

PART II

Me (right) in uniform, from my time in the army.

5.

TRAVEL

I WORKED FOR MONSIEUR PAUL FOR THREE YEARS AND loved all of it. He was disciplined without being a screamer. He didn't try to crush the apprentices. He was a gentleman—very unusual then.

When I was eighteen, I had to serve in the army, as everyone did at the time. I'd cooked with Monsieur Paul at the Élysée Palace in Paris, residence of then-president Valéry d'Estaing, and when Monsieur Paul asked if I wanted him to write a letter requesting that I do my service there, I told him no. I didn't want to be stuck inside. *I wanted to travel.* I wanted to be on a boat, on the sea. So he helped me get stationed on a boat, where I would cook for three officers and the captain as we sailed the Atlantic and the Mediterranean. (The ship carried around 250 men, but other chefs cooked for them in a different kitchen; I alone cooked for the officers.)

After my six months of basic training in Bordeaux I took a train north, arriving in Brest an hour before we pushed off, and I hadn't eaten. I didn't know that this was a recipe for seasickness. I immediately became very sick.

I could barely get out of bed to do the nightly fire drills. During the second drill, I threw up in my mask till there was puke up to my eyeballs. No matter how many times I scrubbed that mask, every time I put it on, that whole year, I smelled that vomit.

I was so sick I eventually threw up blood. They almost had to call a helicopter to take me to shore. But on the seventh day, I woke up, cooked myself some eggs, and I was good to go. The officers were mad at me for being sick. They'd been so excited to have a cook from a Michelin three-star, and all I had done was lie in bed and throw up. Still, they were glad to have me when I was back on my feet and at the stove.

And so was I. I didn't learn much about food and cooking on the ship—I was all by myself, cooking what I already knew. I cooked for four guys for a year. I got them the best of everything—Bresse chickens, langoustines, *fine de claire* oysters. They'd never had such quality. But I knew quality from Monsieur Paul and from *Maman*.

Again, I didn't really grow as a cook, from a technique standpoint. But I tried to perfect what I knew—and I was traveling for the first time in my life. Travel opened my mind and my palate. It began a lifetime of love of travel that has been invaluable to me as a chef, as it should be to you. And I discovered countless ingredients I'd never seen before.

Our first stop was in the Azores, the archipelago west of Portugal. We hit Portugal, Tunisia, Nigeria, Morocco. Casablanca, I thought, "Are you kidding?" I remember every smell, every new ingredient. I'd never seen lemon confit before, or harissa. The cumin was so powerful, it has stayed with me, even all these years later. I have a dish today on the ABC Kitchen menu, carrots with cumin, that is a direct result of that trip in 1976. Fresh ginger was new to me, and fresh olives that had yet to be cured.

We stopped in Portsmouth, England, where I had my first fish and chips. And in Hamburg, Germany. Here I learned to drink and to smoke pot (it was the mid-1970s, after all). I met girls in every port. It was magnificent.

The ports, however, were also a lot of work. I had to completely restock the boat. I learned that if I packed the oysters under a heavy bed of ice, so that they couldn't open easily, they'd stay good for more than a week. In fact, the food I made was too good. The captain loved it so much that in every port they'd have parties every night, and I had to cook for these parties. As far as the cooking went, I loved to be at sea, because I only had four people to cook for.

I won't say that military service was a waste of time, though it felt like it. By the end I was simply biding my time. The officers were so sad to see me go, they nearly cried. I'd done well by them, thanks to Monsieur Paul and my mother. But for me personally, the biggest impact of that year was that it opened up the world. Now I needed to see more new places, new cultures. I knew I had to travel.

I also, however, needed a job. I called Monsieur Paul and asked if I could come back. I was still writing letters to his daughter, and when I returned we no longer kept our relationship a secret.

Once back in my own country, my home, in the kitchen of Auberge, I quickly realized that I couldn't stay long. I was too restless to see more of the world. Monsieur Paul was happy that I was dating his daughter and wanted me to stay. I could have remained for good there if I'd wanted to. But his son had taken a bigger role in the kitchen (and I don't think he liked that I was with his sister). Mainly, though, travel had changed me. I'd changed. After Tunis and Casablanca, I had no desire to be stuck in rural France for the rest of my life.

I set my sights on the south of France, on a restaurant called Moulin de Mougins, run by a respected raconteur and bon vivant chef, Roger Vergé. He'd recently published the influential book *Ma Cuisine de Soleil,* "My Cuisine of the Sun." With his engaging manner and grand mustache, he was a magnetic figure. He was the Matisse of cooking—his style was so bright and whimsical. Also, unlike so many other three-star chefs, he had not come out of Fernand Point's La Pyramide; he was outside the so-called chef mafia, a self-made chef, and this I found impressive. Most of all, I was eager to learn a new palate, to work with the produce and herbs of the south of France. My mind was set for Vergé.

When I reached him, he told me he could have a place for me—in a year. I was upset, of course, because I couldn't spend another whole year in Alsace, let alone settle there. His daughter was going to put the handcuffs on me. I had to leave Auberge. My spirit was already elsewhere. But in retrospect, Vergé's turning me down proved to be a positive thing. More than that, even. The kitchen where I landed would change my life—not just my cooking but the trajectory of my career. Sometimes opportunity can lie within disappointment.

6.

BE OPEN TO
UNFAMILIAR STYLES

THE CHEF LOOKED AT ME WHEN I FIRST ARRIVED IN THE new kitchen and said, "You're the guy from Haeberlin?"

I nodded.

He pointed to the changing room and said, "I just want you to know that whatever you learned at Auberge, forget it. Whatever we show you, that's how you do it. You do it our way. I've seen this before. You think you're from a three-star restaurant and your way is best? Forget it."

This was my new chef, Louis Outhier, at the restaurant L'Oasis, in the town of Mandelieu-la-Napoule, a few miles outside Cannes, between Saint-Tropez and Nice in the south of France. He was a young, dashing chef, impeccably dressed, and he kept his kitchen equally pristine.

Right away I didn't like this kitchen. So strange and unfamiliar. The restaurant was closed on the day I arrived, so I had time to check into a hotel and get my bearings. I still remember walking into the kitchen on my first day. There were cooks there, but they weren't doing anything. Nothing was happening. No one seemed to be working. There were no stocks simmering on the stove tops. I introduced myself to one of the cooks and said, "What, are you closed today?"

He said, "No, we're starting in ten minutes."

It was then that I learned that we were not allowed to start cooking until the first guest *arrived*. We could not even mince a shallot before an order was placed. I couldn't believe it. Outhier arrived at eleven-fifteen. It was his habit to go to his office first and have a cup of tea. If he saw anyone doing anything, he'd freak out: "What are you doing?! Why are you cooking that—no one's ordered it!"

Outhier did have a pedigree from La Pyramide, and he had worked alongside Jean Troisgros and Paul Bocuse under the legendary Fernand Point. But instead of giving him credit for that, I also saw it as his having had one leg up, unlike the independent Vergé, who had made it all on his own. Nevertheless, I had no idea exactly how lucky I was to find myself in Outhier's kitchen. He was a chef ahead of his time.

Monsieur Paul had taught me precision and cleanliness. Through repetition, as well as necessity, I had also learned speed. I'd learned the fundamentals of every part of the three-star kitchen, from pastry to garde-manger, fish, meat, and sauces. During my year-long travels throughout Europe, the Mediterranean, and North Africa, my mind had been alert to new ingredients and flavors. And so I had the tools I needed to learn an entirely new way of cooking, one that, in many ways, was very old and, strangely, more aligned with the cooking of my youth than that of a traditional Michelin three-star.

At Auberge de l'Ill, cooking was all about *mise en place,* everything in its place, everything set up beforehand

and ready to go. Shallots minced, onions sliced, parsley chopped. That's your *mise en place*—everything you need in order to get the job done. The very things aspiring chefs learn in culinary school today. We roasted bones and caramelized onions and simmered stock on the stove top for hours. Monsieur Paul believed that the basics were not just about a superlative product but also about bringing out the essence of those products (such as soaking the cracked pits in the cherry juice). Big pots would simmer for hours on the stoves at Auberge, to make brown veal stock, sauce espagnole and demi-glace, as well as all the individual derivative sauces made from these for each particular bird and cut of meat.

Then I arrived at L'Oasis, and the chef didn't want *anything* on the stove until the customer sat down. He didn't allow you to chop any herbs in advance. Shallots could be peeled, but they had to be minced to order. *Everything* was done *à la minute*. So, for instance, if asparagus with morels was on the menu, the morels were brushed clean, the shallots were peeled, and the asparagus were trimmed but could not be peeled. When an order came in, you peeled the asparagus and put them in the pot. You would then mince and sweat your shallots and put your morels in the pan, and you would do it this way for every single order.

We had no mother stocks, no demi-glace. Stocks were *à la minute*. On the meat station, you roasted a pigeon, leaving the breast on the bone (the legs were confited, which, of course, meant that they could only be prepared ahead of time). You took the roasted pigeon from the oven, chopped the wings, chopped the neck. You roasted the bones in the pan, you deglazed with wine, and you added the Madeira port reduction. You couldn't do the reductions ahead of time, and even here Outhier was insistent on the way a reduction was made. It had to be made in thirds. You weren't permitted to pour a bottle of wine into a pan and set it over a low flame. You had to add a third of a bottle, reduce it, add the second third and reduce it, then add the rest. He could tell if you tried to cut corners and reduce it all in one go. And then to finish the sauce, you simply added water. This brought all the flavors out and blended them, resulting in a sauce with a very clean, roasted flavor, a light delicious sauce, rather than a sticky, gelatinous sauce with a back flavor of bones. I hadn't seen this in a restaurant kitchen before. Water. Outhier used water as his base.

This was not a new idea. The year was 1977. Bernard Loiseau had been gaining attention as chef of La Côte d'Or, in the town of Saulieu in Burgundy. He was a proponent of nouvelle cuisine, and he was working toward a style that was lighter than the traditional French cuisine of the time. He made bold pronouncements about cooking with water, *cuisine à l'eau*. He believed that water should be the base of the sauces as well, rather than the traditional rich roasted veal stock. Some of his three-star colleagues made fun of him for it. Bocuse himself, the Man, walking along the river Seine with the Troisgros brothers, swept his hand out at the river coursing by and said, "Bernard would cry, to see so much sauce going to waste!"

But Loiseau wasn't wrong, as I learned from Outhier.

Outhier was Mr. Clean. He was so precise and elegant in his appearance and demeanor. I found this very impressive. The kitchen was cleaner than the dining room. I loved that. People said he was crazy. He made you change your jacket if you got a single small stain on it. We cleaned all the copper ourselves, using a mixture of Ajax, flour, salt, egg whites, and lemon juice. Everything in that kitchen had to shine.

Every morning we went to the market in Cannes. This was new for me. At Auberge de l'Ill, everything came to the restaurant—the hunters, the farmers, the butcher, the fishmonger, they brought their products to us. There *was* no market. In the south of France, it was different. At the market I found figs and olives and mesclun greens, rosemary and thyme. *Tomatoes.* I had rarely seen a tomato in Alsace. Maybe in the summer someone would slice some up for the staff meal, but we didn't cook with them or use them in restaurant dishes. Here I tasted a ripe tomato for the first time.

I began in the kitchen as a *commis,* an assistant, among some twenty-five chefs. There was a wide range to these cooks. Some were in their forties and would be lifelong cooks in the trenches. Others, like me, were young and ambitious, working the vast ranges. The kitchen was so clean and beautiful. Unlike the enclosed, claustrophobic space I'd been used to at Auberge, here the windows were open and warm breezes swept through, along with the sounds of chirping crickets and the smell of wildflowers. It was a beautiful environment, the south of France.

I learned the new kitchen's ways. How to open a scallop. How to peel an apple. I couldn't believe it. I had been peeling an apple wrong. I'd always peeled around the apple. Outhier wanted apples peeled from pole to pole, so that the wedges weren't marked with ridges. Everything was done for a reason.

Service was intense. But all this *à la minute* cooking was possible because there were so many cooks. No one was responsible for more than two dishes during each service. As a *commis*, I did everything asked of me. Chop the parsley, pass it on. Cook the vegetables, pass them on. The lobsters were blanched alive, the meat was removed from the shell, and I chopped the shell to begin the sauce. All to order.

Outhier personally cooked all the meat—duck, squab, lamb—and he finished all the sauces. When the squab came out of the oven, I'd retrieve a clean copper pan and send the squab to the dining room for presentation; then it would be returned for slicing, while Outhier prepared the sauce.

I had to keep his ramekins of salt filled to just the right level all night long. He was crazy about this. He didn't want his fingers to touch either the sides or the bottom of a ramekin, so I had to constantly monitor his salt, keeping it at a precise level.

Above his stove, he had eight bottles of wines and liqueurs for his sauces. I had to make sure that they were always in exactly the same order so he wouldn't have to look when he reached for one. He knew that the bottle second from the right was the port. If I mixed up the bottles, he might deglaze with the Chartreuse, not the port. The sauce would be ruined and he'd be furious with me. Also, I had to keep the bottles corked just so, with the cork pressed into the bottle about a quarter inch. This way they remained sealed, but Outhier could remove the cork with his thumb and pour in one motion. And I would have to retrieve the cork, return it to the bottle just so, and place the bottle in its proper spot.

The food was amazing. He roasted a whole kidney, and it was a time-consuming preparation. He would season it, and I would put a pan on the stove for him with a pat of butter so that right when he needed it, the butter would be foaming, and he would lay the kidney in the pan and the pan in the oven. It was my job to carefully scrape off the blood that would slowly squeeze out of the kidney as it roasted—he didn't want the blood in the pan. I'd flip the kidney and continue to scrape the blood off it until it was perfectly roasted.

Again, his use of fresh herbs, vinaigrettes, and *à la minute* cooking put him ahead of his time.

As the season wound down and business at the restaurant slowed, I would be allowed to cook more. One of his famous dishes was a turbot soufflé. This was a difficult dish because of all the components and the cooking times—the soufflé had to rise perfectly just as the turbot within finished cooking.

When a turbot soufflé order was called, I'd put a copper pan on the stove. I would mince the shallots, sweat them, add tomato *concassé*—peeled, diced tomato—to the pot, then deglaze the pan with champagne. These were the aromatics and flavors for the soufflé base. I'd lay the turbot in the pot and cook it halfway, remove it, then add the fish fumet and reduce it. I'd add the cream and reduce the sauce again. Then, taking the pan off the heat, I'd add the egg yolk. Meanwhile, I had to make the meringue for the soufflé to fold into the base. Even this wasn't easy the Outhier way. To make a meringue by hand, you have to whip the egg whites vigorously with a whisk. But Outhier didn't want the whisk to touch the bowl. He couldn't stand the raspy clicking of the whisk on metal. Also, the scraping of the metal can discolor the whites. So I had to whip them making no more noise than a *pfft-pfft-pfft* as I brought the egg whites to peaks. Try it and you'll see: *very* difficult without touching the bowl.

To finish the dish, a crouton went onto the service dish, topped with mushroom duxelles, and the partially cooked turbot went on top of this. I'd fold the meringue into the soufflé base and cover the fish with it, sprinkle the top with Parmesan, and pop it into the oven. By the time the soufflé had risen and cooked, the turbot would be just right. An exquisite preparation, tasting of champagne and fresh turbot and fumet, encased in a delicate soufflé. An *amazing* dish.

One of Outhier's foie gras dishes was both ingenious and artful. It came to the table looking like a peach. He would make a "pit" of almonds. Using an ice cream scoop, he would shape the foie gras around the pit. Then he would carve a small ridge to give the foie gras the form of a peach, and he would paint it yellow-pink with beet juice. He'd prepare a *chaud-froid* for the sauce using a chicken *glaçage* flavored with port, and he would make a stem using black truffles and some actual peach leaves. It looked exactly like a peach. Beautiful, fascinating food.

But more important than discovering new dishes and new techniques was this: I learned how to start with nothing. To cook from nothing each day. No stocks, no fumet, nothing. And I was ready. Because in many ways Outhier's method returned me to the food of my number one mentor, my mother. It was a lot like the way she cooked, everything *à la minute.*

SALADE D'ÉTÉ

- Mesclun
  Assaisonnement à part

- champignons + citron, persil
- Avocat + citron, persil
- Amandes + Langoustes + citron, persil.
- Artichauds + citron, persil

Loup en Croûte FERNAND POINT

1 Loup de 1 Kg 700 à 2 Kg (pour 4 personnes) Four 200°
                                                    20 minutes

Pâte à Loup	Pâte du dessous	
1 Kg de Beurre	3 Kg Farine	Bien Frémir
3 Kg de Farine	300 g Beurre	Farine + Beurre
80 g Sel	1 L ½ eau	puis l'eau
10 g sucre		
20 jaunes d'œuf		
1 Litre eau		

A page from my recipe notebook when I was at L'Oasis:
a simple summer salad, and *loup en croûte* from Fernand
Point. The drawing was exactly how I was to decorate
the simple crust of flour, butter, and water. Inside was
a filet of the fish and a mousse made from the fish.
I've done this exact dish recently—it's beautiful.

7.

LOOK, LISTEN, LEARN

AFTER TWO YEARS AT L'OASIS WITH LOUIS OUTHIER, IT was time to move on. At that age, two years is a good time to spend at a single restaurant. As you get older and have more basic knowledge of technique and products, you can learn more quickly. I was twenty-one and ready for a new kitchen.

I'd met Paul Bocuse at Auberge de l'Ill. Monsieur Paul and Bocuse were friends. So it wasn't difficult for me to land a position at the famed Restaurant Paul Bocuse in Lyon. What aspiring chef wouldn't want to work under this man, the most powerful link to Fernand Point and La Pyramide and the most famous chef in Europe, if not the world?

So I went from austere L'Oasis, with its emphasis on fresh, *à la minute* cooking, cooking with water, back to the vats of stock and classical French cuisine I'd been so familiar with. Because of Bocuse's fame, his restaurant did a steady year-round business, serving lunch and dinner. L'Oasis, on the French Riviera, was seasonal, slowing down as the year moved into fall, but Bocuse was busy all the time.

And we made all the traditional dishes. His famous truffle consommé arrived beneath a dome of puff pastry; when you broke through the crust, a cloud of truffle vapor hit you—it was beautiful. Veal Orloff. *Poularde de Bresse en vessie,* a Bresse chicken cooked in a pig's bladder. This particular dish was my territory. I blew up fifty bladders every day, and I smelled like them. After work, I couldn't get anywhere *near* a girl like that. But it's a famous preparation—all the flavors and the gelatin stay within the chicken because of the bladder. Truffles are slipped beneath the skin to make it intensely aromatic. It's still a vital part of the menu there today.

It was in this kitchen that I first learned to work as part of a larger team. There was so much to do, you had no choice. Most importantly, I learned to delegate. I was a *commis,* an assistant, and yet I had two chefs under me, because I couldn't do everything—prep the chicken, man the rotisserie, make the sauces, prepare the dishes to be presented and carved tableside.

In the morning, Chef Paul would take a couple of us to the market, to teach us to shop. This was important. We didn't shop the way non-chefs did. We had to find the perfect produce, yes, but we had to do it *fast*. We had to get back to the kitchen. Bocuse would turn over ten cases of tomatoes, and we'd have to learn to spot the best ones as quickly as possible, because next we'd have to go on to the mushrooms, and so on.

In each kitchen, you learn something completely new and different. This was how you trained and learned then, and it would remain this way through the 1980s: chefs had to come to France to work or attend a culinary school. Now there's less of a need to travel to France, in large measure because the French fundamentals have become almost universal. You don't learn the Italian fundamentals or the Spanish fundamentals. This is likely because the French, specifically Auguste Escoffier, born in 1846, codified the fundamentals, and because they work. Whether you're in America or Singapore, beginning culinary students learn French fundamentals.

I'd been at Bocuse for about ten months when a chef who had worked with Monsieur Paul *and* with Bocuse came to eat at the restaurant. Eckart Witzigmann. He was a brilliant Austrian chef, and his Munich restaurant, Aubergine, had just been given three Michelin stars. He saw me in the kitchen, and after dinner, he came to talk to me. "I need you," he said. "I've just lost five cooks."

This was a great opportunity for me, and I'd learned what I needed at this ultratraditional restaurant. But Bocuse wasn't going to like it. I hadn't even been there a year. I said to Eckart, "You tell Bocuse."

Eckart was nearly forty at the time. He said, "That's *your* issue."

It took me a week to work up the courage to knock on Chef Paul's door. As soon as he saw me, he said, "You're leaving."

I said, "How did you know?"

He said, "I saw you talking with Eckart."

Then he screamed at me. How could I leave before a year was out? he shouted. He was very angry, and he let me know it. I couldn't tell if I was allowed to go or not.

You don't want to make an enemy of Paul Bocuse. You always want to leave a kitchen on good terms no matter where you are.

A few days later, he took me to the market with him to shop, and he apologized for screaming at me. He was a gentleman. Then he said, "You can go in two weeks."

I didn't say anything.

"I can see it in your eyes," he continued. "When a cook wants to leave, their head is not in it anymore."

And so I left Restaurant Paul Bocuse, after eleven months, for Munich. Here, in this city, I felt very comfortable. Strasbourg, the largest city near my hometown, is on the German border and is as much German in feel as it is French. I didn't even learn to speak French until I was five and began school. Up till then I spoke Alsatian, a German patois.

Eckart was an amazing chef and cook, but he was crazy. His restaurant was both exciting and nerve-racking. Eckart waited every day to see what the available meat and produce looked like; he let the ingredients tell him what to cook—what he felt like cooking, what inspired him. We'd work from ten a.m. till midnight, but for the first six hours we could only do the most basic preparations; we would sharpen our knives and look at what was being delivered. We would know we had turbot, we had langoustines, but we couldn't touch them until Eckart decided what the menu was. He wouldn't post the night's menu until four p.m. So there was very little we could do until he put that menu up. And then we'd have to hustle. At L'Oasis, the cooking could be more structured because Outhier would have the same items on the menu for two weeks. Not Eckart. Just before service, he would come around to all of our stations and demo the dish as he wanted it. The fileted fish preparation was different every day. If it was a roasted fish, it would be roasted on the bone, and then the bone would be used to make an *à la minute* fumet. This way of working was hard, but because of my training under Outhier, I was more than equal to last-minute cooking, preparing a new selection of dishes every night. I still have every one of those menus.

Each night after service, after we were finished cleaning the kitchen, he made all of us go out and drink beer and talk about food. He'd grill us on what we'd cooked at all of the restaurants we'd worked at. I didn't always want to do this, because I was so exhausted, but I realize now that he was firing our imaginations, sparking his own imagination. He was getting ideas. Because he was the youngest chef to earn three Michelin stars, he had fleets of new chefs coming from all over to work for him. "How did you do the foie gras there?" he'd ask. And we'd all talk about it. One night he asked me, What was the best fish dish at Outhier? I described the turbot soufflé, and he wanted to hear all the details. We'd cook all day and clean the kitchen, then talk about cooking late into the night. Two weeks later, a version of Outhier's turbot soufflé appeared on Eckart's menu.

*

YOU MUST LEARN as much as you can from every kitchen you work in. At Monsieur Paul's, I of course learned how to properly cook a green vegetable, how to glaze (never use sugar—there is plenty of sugar in a root vegetable for proper glazing, to achieve that enticing sheen), how to determine the doneness of a large cut of meat by touch, and on and on.

But you also learn by watching. I learned so much simply by watching Monsieur Paul prepare the foie gras. At this he was a master and a monk. He would make the foie gras after the lunch service, after the kitchen was cleaned, when the cooks were taking their break and the kitchen was quiet. It was his form of meditation.

Before lunch, one of us would set the goose liver out to temper—it came wrapped in paper back then, not sealed in plastic—so that it would be pliable, not hard from the refrigerator. Every day I asked if I could help, if I could watch, but he always said no. It was one of the first dishes of his I'd tasted, as a sixteen-year-old, and I knew that I would never forget it. So I had to learn how he did it.

I kept asking, because he was famous for his foie gras preparations. I think he eventually got tired of my begging and finally let me in to watch.

He first carefully separated the two lobes, the smaller from the larger, connected by a network of veins. He removed the veins with his fingers alone. He simply slid his finger down the foie gras, finding each tributary and gently pulling it out. Veins in the liver will be red with blood and unsightly even after the meat is cooked, so it's important to remove them. Most people use the tip of a paring knife. He didn't even use this; he simply lifted each vein with a fingernail and gently tugged it out of the lobe. It was slow and painstaking, but he never hurried. He knew the liver's vein structure so well, I think he could have done it blindfolded. When he finished, he had scarcely opened up the lobe at all. Eventually, because I went to watch him every day I could, he taught me.

When the lobes were deveined, he covered a sheet pan with parchment paper; then he seasoned the parchment with salt and white pepper, so that when he laid the liver down, the pan would season that side of it. He wouldn't turn the foie gras over—he set it in the pan once and didn't touch it again. He seasoned the side facing up with salt and pepper and gave it a drizzle of kirsch. And then perhaps some late-harvest gewürztraminer. He would never open a new bottle; he would just use what was left from a bottle at lunch.

Then he would cover the pan with a towel, a *torchon,* and let it sit for an hour and a half. When the salt had time to dissolve and the seasoning had begun to penetrate, he lay the foie gras in a terrine mold, covered it with foil, and baked it in a water bath at perhaps 300°F for fifty minutes. Then he let it cool before putting it in the cooler. Here it would stay for five days. Monsieur Paul never served it the same day or even the next. If he made the foie gras on Monday, it wouldn't be ready until Friday.

He would do many things with the foie gras. Often he served it simply—cold with some brioche. Sometimes he stuffed it with truffles and baked it in a crust, *foie gras en croûte.* This was the traditional Alsatian preparation. Here, because the foie gras shrinks somewhat, and the crust puffs up, there was another step. He made small holes in the crust to let the steam out and then, when it was cold, he would pour a very gelatinous beef stock in to fill all the gaps. It would solidify so that the *foie en croûte* could be sliced. Few chefs do this anymore, with the truffles in the middle. (Monsieur Paul froze his truffles so that he could serve them all year round.) He cooked his foie perfectly, just till it was barely done. Too often, foie gras is overcooked and becomes gray. His was always rosy. They were all beautiful dishes.

Sometimes he served the foie gras in a terrine, table-side. The server would carefully spoon out two perfect quenelles and plate them for the diner, along with some toasted brioche—so simple and elegant.

He also made what he called "truffle surprise." He formed foie gras around a truffle. Around this, he molded a thin, fatty pork forcemeat. Then he wrapped it in puff pastry and deep-fried it. Oh my God, that was so good. That was my favorite of all his preparations.

But it wasn't the elaborate *foie gras en croûte* or the truffle surprise that impressed me the most. Looking back now, I see that it was the attitude and care Monsieur Paul brought to the deveining and seasoning of the raw foie gras that had the strongest influence on me. I will never forget the quiet, the patience, the elegance of his fingers as he traced the course of the veins to remove them. From him I learned the grace of this work.

*

IN EACH KITCHEN, four of them from the age of sixteen till age twenty-two—Auberge de l'Ill, L'Oasis, Paul Bocuse, and Aubergine—I learned different facets of the culinary arts. From Monsieur Paul I learned not only the basics of, well, everything—pastry, garde-manger, butchery, sauces—but also things other chefs didn't know, or know at his level: the foie gras, for instance, and how to evaluate caviar. He had studied under a chef who had cooked for the Russian czar, a chef who knew caviar, and he, in turn, taught me how to evaluate it, what color it should be, how to press the eggs against your palate to sense how much fat is in them. This is how culinary knowledge spreads. I learned the basics with Monsieur Paul and earned my certificate. At L'Oasis, I learned the *à la minute* cooking of Outhier, who, strangely, returned me to the cooking of my mother, of my youth.

From Bocuse I learned the deeply traditional dishes that dated back to Fernand Point and his La Pyramide. I learned how to evaluate the raw ingredients. He always got the best of everything. I will never forget how he would turn over ten boxes of tomatoes to pick the very best ones, carefully picking through the cèpes. He could do this because he was the pope of Lyon, the city's most famous citizen. He put Lyon on the map. His influence is ubiquitous in that city—you see his image everywhere. He was a genius at promotion and is largely credited with ushering chefs into their current celebrity status. He brought chefs out of the kitchen. He was a great chef and a great man, one whose influence on our industry can hardly be overstated.

At Aubergine, I learned how to work with a team, everyone sharing their history, their stories, the dishes from their chefs, and ideas from their own imaginations to create a truly dynamic and exciting kitchen dedicated to preparing a new menu every day.

Everywhere, you learn. Always be learning. Never stop learning.

Egg Caviar for Two

If there is a single dish that represents my time with Louis Outhier, it's egg caviar, the simplest of preparations—egg, cream, and caviar—which I first prepared at L'Oasis in the 1970s. It is still on my menu today. Forty years later. Think about that. Forty years and it's still one of the most popular dishes on my menus. If there's a dish at any of my restaurants that's close to perfection, this is it, in its look, its textures, and the intertwining flavors. And it remains one of my personal favorites—caviar on gently scrambled eggs with a savory, vodka-spiked cream, served in a hollowed-out eggshell. It remains a pleasure to make, and it remains a pleasure to eat. People smile when the dish is presented to the table. Eggs on eggs, served in an eggshell. (If you don't want to serve it in an eggshell, serve it in a small egg cup or an espresso cup.) Egg caviar is still on the menu at Jean-Georges, and when I opened the Dempsey Cookhouse and Bar in Singapore last year, I put it on the menu there as well. This dish is timeless.

No step is difficult—scrambled eggs are topped with cream and caviar, and that's it. So the critical cooking point of this recipe is scrambling the eggs. Scrambled eggs are one of the most overcooked dishes in the United States, both in homes and in the buffet steam-table inserts at hotels throughout the country. To me, they epitomize mediocrity and thoughtlessness in the kitchen. In fact, scrambled eggs can and should be one of the most special dishes you can make. The curds should be delicate and moist and coated with egg that's warm and thickened but still fluid.

At the restaurants, we take the extra step of cutting off the tops of the eggshells, boiling the bottom of the shells for a minute or two, then carefully removing the membrane. This makes for a four-star serving. But the important part of this dish is really the dish itself, caviar on very soft scrambled eggs and the seasoned cream.

First, make the cream:

> ½ cup whipping cream
> ¼ teaspoon salt
> Pinch of cayenne

Put these ingredients in a bowl and whip them till the cream reaches the point of gentle but stiff peaks.

> 1 teaspoon vodka
> 1 teaspoon lemon juice

Add the vodka and lemon juice to the whipped cream, whip it again, and taste it. Add more lemon if needed. The cream should taste seasoned, not salty. Remember, the caviar is salty—that's the main salt in this dish. The cream should have some piquancy from the cayenne, but it shouldn't be spicy. And it shouldn't taste lemony—it should have just a little acidity to balance the richness of the cream. (At the restaurants, we now add a pinch of xanthan gum to ensure a good, stable consistency, but that's optional. Outhier wouldn't have even heard of xanthan gum.)

Put the whipped cream in a bag if you intend to pipe it; that is how we do it at the restaurants.

*2 tablespoons unsalted butter, and more as
    needed
2 eggs, blended until uniform
Pinch of salt*

Put two teaspoons of butter in a saucepan over medium-high heat. When it begins to melt, add the eggs and salt. This is very difficult to *describe* in a recipe, in words, but is easy to *show,* so I always, always do it with my cooks to show them. I use about an ounce of egg for each portion, squeezed out of a plastic squeeze bottle into a bartender's two-ounce jigger. That's about half an egg, all you need for this. But if you're making this recipe for four, use four eggs to ensure that you have what you need. Whisk the eggs continuously over the heat until they are thick but still fluid. Regulate the heat by holding the pan on or above the burner. This should take a minute or two. This is the tricky stage, because even after you take the pan off the heat, the eggs will continue to cook. Almost always my young chefs overcook the eggs at first. They don't take into account how much carryover cooking will occur. Remember, you can always put the pan back on the heat.

Remove the eggs from the heat when they are 90 percent cooked but still very fluid, then immediately add some butter, which will help to stop their cooking and cool them down. If I see that they've gone over—and I do this myself, take the eggs too far—I'll add a squeeze of raw egg to obtain the right consistency. When the butter has been fully incorporated into the eggs, you should be able to let the egg fall from a spoon like a thick sauce into the cleaned shells. That's how soft the eggs should be.

> 2 full tablespoons osetra caviar
> 2 cleaned eggshells (or two egg cups or 2
>   espresso cups)

Spoon the eggs into your serving vessel—we use eggshells at the restaurants, but feel free to use anything your imagination might suggest. Pipe about half of the whipped, flavored cream around the edges. Top each egg with a heaping tablespoon of caviar. Serve immediately.

I don't know if there's a better preparation on the planet. Taste it! See for yourself. I've been making a variation of this recipe since the late 1970s. Simplicity itself—three components: egg, cream, caviar. What's good is good, forever.

SERVES 2

BANGKOK

PART III

Miroirs

Intérieur

— 250 gr   amandes en poudre.
— 250 gr   sucre.
— 100 gr   beurre fondu.
— 2   œufs entiers.
— 2   jaunes d'œufs

Extérieure

— 300 gr   Blancs d'œufs.
— 325 gr   sucre
— 325 gr   Amandes en poudre.
— 50 gr   farine

---- pâte extérieure

« Sur la pâte extérieure, on met des amandes Blanchies
effilées. Hachées avant la cuisson et avant de mettre
la pâte intérieure.
Sur la pâte intérieure après la cuisson, on met
dessus du ~~ma~~ nappage. »

Two cookie recipes from my days at L'Oasis—Outhier
cookies. Notice the first one uses egg yolks, and
the second uses egg whites. Notice also how neat
my handwriting is when I can write on a grid!

8.

MAINLINING STREET FOOD

I'D BEEN IN MUNICH AT AUBERGINE FOR ONLY A FEW months when Outhier called me. He wanted me to help him open a restaurant.

In Thailand.

I knew nothing about opening a restaurant. I had never been *the* chef of any restaurant, had never run a kitchen. I had never even been a sous-chef. So far, I had only ever been *chef de partie,* and now I was being asked to be the chef. In a restaurant on the other side of the world. Yes, I was scared. When I told my parents, they said they thought I was crazy to consider it and that they did not want me to go. But I'd had a taste of travel; I knew I didn't want to be bound to Alsace, and not even to Europe. I had to do this. You have to take these kinds of risks in order to grow. But I didn't just grow by accepting the risk. This move would be the defining moment of my career and set my course for the future.

Outhier was well known then, and executives at the Oriental hotel in Bangkok, which housed one of three luxury restaurants in the city, had reached out to see if he'd be interested in taking over the restaurant in their hotel. Outhier, always forward-thinking, wanted to do it.

Outhier's decision to branch out beyond France was the beginning of a broader expansion by chefs that began at this time and took off in the early 1980s. Bocuse, with his fame and gift for promoting chefs, was among the first of the French chefs to expand beyond Europe, opening restaurants in the Far East. Interest in fine dining, food, and restaurants was beginning to grow everywhere. Hotels already had the infrastructure required to open a restaurant. They had a human resources department, accounting personnel, laundry facilities, and so on. They had the space. They needed to offer food. It was much easier for them to hire people who knew how to create and operate restaurants to do it for them, for a cut of the proceeds, than to try to do it themselves. French chefs were the most notable in the world, and the most in demand were Michelin three-star chefs. Outhier and his restaurant were famous, and so when the Oriental hotel executives needed someone to take over an existing restaurant in their hotel, he was an obvious choice.

And so he contacted me, a *chef de partie* in Munich who knew nothing about opening restaurants! I was twenty-three and was ready to take on the challenge. Never say no to a challenge.

*

THE FIRST STEP in his opening a restaurant in Thailand was for me to return to L'Oasis and work there, so that I could return to Outhier's style. I was happy to be away from the big vats of stocks simmering overnight and the deeply traditional fare, the morel cream sauce, those smelly bladders! And back to the spare, clean style of Outhier.

However, I was there not to cook for the restaurant but to develop the menu for his restaurant at the Oriental. I needed to be there to cook with Outhier so that I would know exactly what he wanted in each dish. The task was relatively simple; we were doing only twelve dishes—six first courses, six main courses—and straightforward desserts. But they were all familiar in style, classical three-star French dishes—salmon mille-feuille, turbot soufflé.

This was also a chance for Outhier to learn what I'd learned. He would say, Cook me something from Bocuse. Cook me something from Witzigmann. For six months I cooked this way, and when our menu was set, I boarded a plane for Thailand. I wasn't alone. Outhier was also sending along a fellow chef my age, Bertrand, who was to help me open the restaurant and manage a kitchen staff of twenty cooks.

Nothing could have prepared me for the shock of this new land.

I'd really never spent any time outside of Europe, other than some port stops in North Africa. I'd never been in a jungle. I'd never tasted Chinese food, let alone Thai food. There weren't any Asian restaurants in Alsace in the 1970s.

I'll never forget stepping off the plane and getting smacked with the hot, humid air of Thailand and the wild smell of the place. This was before the prevalence of jetways. These days, when you arrive in a foreign land, you walk straight from the plane into an air-conditioned airport—you could be anywhere. Not so in 1980 when I arrived in Bangkok. I stepped through the doorway of the plane into pungent air that smelled of jungle and rot. Aromas of lemongrass and durian and fermented fish.

Bertrand and I got our bags and were met by a driver who would take us to our hotel. We weren't in the car for ten minutes when we passed a market on the side of the road and I smelled cooking. We asked the driver to pull over. He said, "I have to take you to the hotel." We told him the hotel could wait. I went to the first stall I saw.

The guy there was selling some kind of soup—he was a street vendor, a street cook (the original food truck!). But he wasn't just ladling soup into a cup; he was making it from scratch. He poured water into a small pot—filthy water from a jerrican, but water. He threw in some stalks of something I'd never seen, some leaves I'd never seen, as the water came to a simmer. He shook some liquid from a bottle into it, squeezed lime into it. When it had simmered for a minute or two, he put some shrimp and mushrooms in. I didn't know what most of this stuff was. I didn't even cook with limes at this point—we didn't use *limes* in Alsace.

When the shrimp was cooked, he poured it all into a bowl. I handed him some French francs, the only money I had. And I ate.

My life changed at that moment.

I tasted the lemongrass, though I had no idea what it was. I tasted lime. The soup was *acidic*. I had grown up with acidity—my mother had taught me this. But never in soup! The fire, the heat of the chilies—I'd never known any of this. And something like lime but better, more fragrant, lime distilled into perfume. Amazing. And the shrimp, perfectly cooked. And the mushrooms, so springy in the broth. I had never had these mushrooms before, never anything remotely like any of this.

My head all but exploded. This was not the world I knew.

I motioned to the guy, miming, "Where can I get more food?" He pointed down the road. We departed. At the next stall I had a coconut curry soup. I hadn't known that coconut milk *existed*. Street food. *Amazing*. Today, a version of that coconut soup, the one I had on the side of the road during my first moments in Bangkok, is on the menu at Mercer Kitchen in New York. But back then, all of this was novel, and so Bertrand and I moved on to the next stall.

Down the road, another guy made green papaya salad. Unripe papaya—I'd never heard of using this. He ground chilies and seasoning and herbs in a mortar. He tossed it with lime juice and fish sauce. I tasted—*boom*. The lime juice, along with the heat of fresh chilies and another flavor, a beguiling one I couldn't place—the fish sauce. Here were dried shrimp, something else I'd never tasted. Coming from France, I knew nothing of chilies and their intense heat, the sweetness of palm sugar, the basil and mint.

I wanted more, and then more. It was as if the world had been black and white until I tasted that soup, tom yum kung. We made our driver stop five times. After the green papaya salad, we found a curry soup—again, distinct from the other two, and I was astonished. I knew Indian curries, but these curries were utterly different. Even the succulent meat, the scrumptious little morsels—what were they? Definitely not chicken. Did it look, I wondered, a little like rabbit? I tried to ask what the meat was, but I couldn't understand what the guy cooking it said. I didn't care, it tasted so good and so new. Turmeric, and galangal, and coconut milk—delicious. (It would be six months before I discovered what the meat was: *water rats*. Water rats infest the rice patties—so they're relatively clean, not like New York City rats. I highly recommend!)

It's impossible to convey to you the dizzying effect of all these new flavors, the pungent smells of jungle and rot and chilies and ginger and smoke, against the backdrop of the pagoda temples. I'd read about these temples, but this was before the Internet, and so I'd never actually seen one or even a picture of one. And the Buddhists, I'd never seen them before, either. They didn't look like altar boys. Buddhism was the main religion there, and it was my first experience of faiths outside the Western tradition. I also learned that the best markets were always near the Buddhist temples. Seriously—if you want good food in Southeast Asia, find the nearest temple and there's sure to be the best food right nearby.

Absolute. Culture. Shock. I was electrified.

*

THAT FIRST NIGHT Bertrand and I went out and we got crazy, partying, so excited to be in this strange land. And the next day we began to start organizing the restaurant.

Outhier had sent me with the agreement that I was going to be the chef and that my fellow chef, Bertrand, was there to help me. As I've mentioned, I hadn't even been a sous-chef yet. Now I was to be the chef. I was scared and green. Fortunately or not, he'd told Bertrand the exact same thing. That *he* was to be the chef, and *I* was there to help. We were both a little pissed, but Outhier's strategy had been shrewd. It was so new for both of us, and we were both more scared than irritated, and so we both wanted to make it work.

Unfortunately, Bertrand went out again the next night and again went crazy. He seemed to go out every night after that, living on one hour of sleep. It was not a sustainable schedule, and eventually he became a wreck. I loved the nightlife of Bangkok. There was all kinds of trouble to be found. Opium dens, for instance. Well, as a chef, I felt obligated to at least try an opium den. *Crazy.* I can see why people get lost for two days. Opium is so strong you can hardly move. It's a danger in our industry all cooks should take seriously. It helped to take down my old chef at Aubergine eventually—Eckart was convicted of cocaine possession and nearly lost his restaurant. In any case, Bertrand got too deep into the partying scene and Outhier had no choice but to fly him home.

You chefs out there need to be careful. The biggest risk is that you will lose your focus, a focus on what matters in your work, and you simply won't last. I see it in my own kitchens. I see young chefs come back to work after two days off, and they're dragging. I can see why in their eyes, smell it on their breath. When it happens more than once, I talk to them, tell them to stay focused.

In Bangkok, I didn't go crazy, and I didn't party every night. I was too afraid of failing at opening my first restaurant, so I would always be home by one. With Bertrand gone, I was now the executive chef and responsible for whatever happened. The stakes were very high.

Outhier soon rented me a big apartment within walking distance of the hotel. I had a maid, a cook, and a chauffeur. When I returned home from work, a bath was drawn for me. The cook asked if she could prepare me dinner. I always accepted. She taught me Thai home cooking. I was twenty-three and I was living like a king.

*

THIS WAS HOW I BEGAN two years in Thailand—learning, learning, learning. I was one of the youngest people in the kitchen, but the Thai cooks were respectful. And they, too, would cook traditional Thai dishes for me. Every night something new. This was how I learned Thai cooking.

The restaurant was a traditional French restaurant, doing our traditional French standbys. Steak au poivre, steak Diane, salmon sliced on a trolley, everything served tableside. Nothing came to the table on a plate. But it was the 1980s, nouvelle cuisine was in the air, and I knew things were changing.

The Japanese had been a strong influence in that direction. At all the French kitchens, there were many Japanese *stagiaires* and cooks. Sometimes, during my years at Auberge, I brought them home with me, and my mother cooked for them. I watched how they cooked and served. They prepared extraordinarily elegant, plated food. And I believe that their influence was key to the nouvelle cuisine movement in France and then America. We had begun cooking this way at Outhier's L'Oasis. He was one of nouvelle cuisine's progenitors—and I believe it was a direct result of the Japanese cooks who worked in the kitchen.

After a few months, I noticed that nobody liked the menu we were serving. The restaurant was dead. I would call Outhier every day and say, "Chef, last year on this day the restaurant did eighty dinners. This year, fifteen." And the food was good. It was all Outhier, the same food, more or less, that had made him famous in France. But everyone was getting nervous. One night, by good fortune, King Bhumibol Adulyadej bought out the restaurant. King Bhumibol would become the world's longest-ruling monarch and was beloved by the people. He'd been to the restaurant before, long before I'd arrived, and had liked it. So he dined with us and it was front-page news, that the king of Thailand had eaten here. The phones started ringing that day, and they never stopped.

We were full from that night on. I was saved by the king of Thailand! After he ate there, we could cook anything we wanted.

*

COOKING TRADITIONAL French food was difficult in Southeast Asia back then, nearly forty years ago—Western cooking, at least. They had no butter or cream. No dairy at all. How do you cook traditional French food without butter? So Outhier had to ship that in. He also shipped in foie gras, which the Thai adored.

But other staples I took for granted were either hard to find or nonexistent. Carrots and leeks were rare. I had to do without them. They just didn't seem to grow there—I'd have to get my sweetness elsewhere. There was no fennel, no beets, no parsnips, no cèpes. I had to improvise. I was forced to use scallions instead of leeks. I'd never seen a scallion before. It was much more oniony, dense, strong. My mushrooms became straw and shiitake—I liked them;

they were meaty and had great texture. Apples in Thailand were rare, and prohibitively expensive. I couldn't do Outhier's amazing foie gras with apples or his duck with apples and brandy. I'd spent years peeling those apples pole-to-pole, and now I had almost none.

What was I going to pair with foie gras? What fruit *was* available? Mangoes were all over the place. This was a brand-new fruit for me. So ripe the juice dripped down your chin. They were amazingly sweet and tart—not *unlike* apples. Could you, I wondered, pair foie gras with mango? I tried it, and you know what? Mango and foie gras is an *amazing* pairing. Even better than apple! Extraordinary. Forced to improvise, we came up with dishes even better than what we'd originally hoped for.

I ate the street food every day, picking up new foods at the market on my way to the hotel. The Thai chefs cooked for me. The food was electrifyingly good. And yet I still had to make the cream reduction and slice the foie gras. I had to make Outhier's French food. We did the duck with apples that I'd been making since I'd first learned to peel apples the Outhier way. Apples were expensive, and now I knew I could do duck with mango instead. But no—there were limits to what I could change. People came to us for classical French, for the truffles and *sauce Choron*. We had other difficulties, too, and sometimes there was no way to prepare the traditional recipe. I couldn't get the fish I was used to. There was no John Dory here. You couldn't ship fish back then, not to Thailand. So I cooked what was available and discovered a great fish native to those waters, *pla kapong*, like a black sea bass.

After I'd been working in Thailand for six months, Outhier came to visit. I cooked Thai-style food for him, and he loved it. For the restaurant, I was making foie gras with a green apple compote and a sorrel-like herb, and a sauce of calvados and veal *jus* mounted with the fat of the foie gras. When Outhier came, I wanted to show him some of the local flavors. So I made the foie gras, but I did it with a julienne of ginger and vegetable stock, and I finished it with vodka. Vodka and ginger are an amazing pair. And I served it with caramelized mango. It was basically the same dish as the foie gras with apples, but it had a completely different effect.

Outhier was crazy about it. And more: he returned with bags of ginger and galangal and Thai chili paste.

He and I created a Thai lobster dish that he would serve at L'Oasis. We sweated red chili paste in butter, caramelizing it. We added julienned carrots, then white port, and reduced it almost all the way, then used a julienne of green apple and some turmeric for color—that was the base of the sauce. Shortly before serving it, we combined this base with cream and coconut milk and brought it to a simmer. Then we seasoned it with lime juice; this would be the sauce for the poached lobster.

For another dish, we added red chili paste to duck *jus*, along with galangal, garlic, and fish sauce, then combined this with caramel, the sweetness balancing the savory heat. We called it duck *à l'orientale*.

I think we came up with two dozen recipes like this. I was very shy about putting them on the menu of a restaurant that billed itself as classical French. But Outhier had no compunctions about doing it in France. For him, it was the new Outhier.

And diners and even his three-star colleagues embraced it. They saw how he had been inspired by Southeast Asia, and they admired him for it. This was how Outhier became known as the chef who introduced Asian flavors into the nouvelle cuisine.

I was now regularly sending Outhier mango and galangal and lime leaves, as he continued to send me foie gras and cream.

This new freedom to blend cuisines, combined with the need to improvise using Southeast Asian ingredients, my love of Thai food, and Outhier's embrace of Asian ingredients—all this became the seed of the style that would help to distinguish me, though I couldn't have known it then, and to launch me in New York.

All of it really began with the tom yum kung, my first bite in Thailand. That changed everything. When I spoke with Outhier by phone that first week, I told him, "I want to learn everything there is to know about Thai cuisine. I want to eat it for breakfast, lunch, and dinner." And I learned it, so that even while we opened a traditional French restaurant, I embraced all things Thai.

This is how my style of cooking was born, how I found what, arguably, set me apart from the rest of haute cuisine not long after I arrived in New York City and was trashed by Gael Greene in *New York* magazine—but that comes later. That first soup changed my life—me, twenty-three, standing at the roadside in Bangkok eating tom yum kung.

Tom Yum Kung

The soup that changed my life is a lesson in simplicity.

But remember, you have already smelled lemongrass; you have cooked with lime and ginger. I never had. It doesn't take a genius. It takes ingredients. And a trip to another world.

And I want you to make it. It shows you the power of water—from Outhier to Bangkok. So simple, yet I make it for my best chefs today, those who have been with me for years, and still, they taste, they shake their heads and marvel.

So. *Mise en place.* Set your ingredients out in separate bowls:

> *3 cups water*
> *2 stalks lemongrass*
> *6 Kaffir lime leaves*
> *Fish sauce to taste (about 4 teaspoons; we use*
> *   the Red Boat brand)*
> *Lime juice to taste (one juicy lime, 4 teaspoons*
> *   should do)*
> *1 or 2 Thai chilies*
> *½ pound shrimp or 12 large (under 16 count)*
> *   shrimp (for four portions), peeled and*
> *   deveined*

8 small porcini, quartered, or 12 straw
*   mushrooms*
Cilantro for garnish

Don't do anything other than peel the shrimp maybe, and brush off the mushrooms so they're clean. But otherwise you prepare as you go. It comes together quickly.

Put a couple of cups of water in a saucepan—I use Fiji bottled water, but if you have a jerrican of water at your side, that will do—and place it over high heat. Take the two stalks of lemongrass, trim the root ends, cut them into thirds widthwise, and then bruise them deeply with the back of your knife, *whack whack whack,* up and down each section. Smell them. Lemongrass is my favorite ingredient, magical. Bruising it helps release the perfume. Toss the pieces into the water.

Next, the lime leaves. Twist and crush them with your fingers, again bruising them to release the flavors. Add them to the pot as well. The water should be getting hot, and you should be able to smell the citrus. It's like making tea—you're simply steeping these aromatics, not cooking them.

Now rest a bit as the water comes to a simmer. Enjoy the fragrance. Thinly slice the chilies—but be careful, because good Thai chilies are very, very hot. Quarter the mushrooms. I use only one small Thai chili for two cups of water, one stalk of lemongrass per cup, and three lime leaves per cup. A good ratio.

When the water comes to a strong simmer, but before

it begins to boil, turn the heat to low. You don't want it to reduce. You just want to steep the lemongrass and the lime leaves. Already it smells good enough to drink. Once the lemongrass and the lime leaves have steeped for a few minutes and the lime leaves have turned a dull green, it's time to season your soup.

First, add your salt: the fish sauce, *nam pla*. I add it a teaspoon at a time, tasting after each one. For two cups, I like four teaspoons, but it's up to you. Next, acidity: lime juice. Limes have such a stiff core, they can be hard to juice by hand. Cut them into thirds lengthwise, off-center, so that you see only the flesh on the cut face. You basically cut off the sides, leaving a triangle of core.

Now squeeze a couple of the pieces of lime into your pot. Taste. Squeeze some more. It should not make you pucker, but it should be powerfully acidic. Most people err on the side of underseasoning. Taste while you season. Don't follow recipes when it comes to seasoning.

Now, as you're tasting, you're seeing that this is already delicious. Be sure to season with enough lime so that this broth tastes delicious as is. It should be good enough to drink right now: lemongrass, lime leaves, fish sauce, lime juice. The Thai foundation in two cups of water.

And that's it. Add the rest of the ingredients: the finely sliced chili, the shrimp, and the mushrooms. I love to use fresh porcini, because they mimic the texture of the traditional straw mushrooms, but you can also use cremini.

Turn the flame up now, to get the broth back up to a good heat; it will have cooled a little from the addition of the cold shrimp and the mushrooms. The shrimp need only a minute once the broth returns to a simmer.

Take the pot off the heat and taste the liquid. Does it need more fish sauce? If so, add it. Same with the lime.

3 cups steamed jasmine rice (¾ cups per serving)

Serve the soup immediately—the shrimp are still cooking, remember—and tear some of the cilantro leaves over each of the bowls. Serve some rice separately to eat with the soup. That's how they do it in Thailand (and how I serve the coconut soup at Mercer Kitchen).

Taste all the flavors in this broth—mushroom, shrimp, heat, lemongrass, lime, *nam pla*. This is as close as I can bring you to what I experienced on that arrival in Bangkok. But you can never know the wonder I felt, because you have already smelled lemongrass, you have cooked with lime leaves and fish sauce. For me, it was a new world.

Serves 4

9.

FIRST, VISIT THE FOOD MARKETS

AFTER I'D SPENT TEN MONTHS ALONE IN BANGKOK, MY girlfriend, Muriel, whom I'd met while working at L'Oasis, arrived. Because she didn't have a visa, she had to leave the country once a month. I couldn't afford to keep sending her to other countries, so my food and beverage director told me how to fix the problem: get married. And so we did. Not long after that she was pregnant with our first child, Cédric. When Muriel went into labor, we had to take a *tuk-tuk,* a rickshaw, to the hospital.

Life was hard—being a husband and father, and also being in charge of the restaurant. I started the workday by running lunch. Every afternoon, I took English lessons for an hour. Then I returned to the restaurant to run dinner.

And because of all of this—the strenuous work, the responsibilities of being a husband and father—I changed. Up to this point, I'd thought that I had to do everything, even the vinaigrettes. But I couldn't continue to do it all, so I learned to delegate. I learned not simply how to let go of making the vinaigrettes; I went a step further and taught my cooks classical French vinaigrettes. I was twenty-four, and I felt for the first time, after eight years of cooking in the best restaurants in France, and opening a restaurant in this foreign land, that I had become a chef. Which to me now meant that I'd become a leader and, more important, a *teacher*.

*

I WOULD SOON BE moving on, but no place would ever be like Bangkok to me or come close to having the same impact. I loved the beggars, the lepers, the water rats, the funky jungle rot in the air. The intensely sour flavors, the chili heat, the deep fermented umami of *nam pla*.

Every morning when I had time, I walked to work (if I was late, I took a *tuk-tuk*). The route was about a mile, and it sent me straight through Bangkok's main food market. The walk took thirty minutes, about twenty minutes of it within the market. It was a harsh and crowded place, teeming with lepers and beggars and street people and families shopping for food. The streets were lined with stalls, made of bamboo covered with drapery to shield the merchants and their products from the sun. The air was perfumed with lemongrass and lime and coriander and mint by the bushel. All the meat and fish were sold inside the main building. It was oppressively pungent in there: none of the fish were on ice, and flies covered all the meat. Here I saw all that the land and water offered. No beef. No lamb. No goat. Only pork and birds and fish. Fisherman brought in great baskets of live shrimp, all fresh and glistening—but they wouldn't stay that way for long in the heat. Bangkok is on water, the Gulf of Thailand, and I found all kinds of new fish to try, both from the gulf and from the many rivers and canals that run through the city. All manner of herbs and fresh and dried chilies and mushrooms, galangal, curries, the fermented fish sauces and pastes and dried fish were sold here. And a staggering amount of fruit, fruit I'd never seen before, let alone used. Rambutan, a hairy lychee-like fruit, dragon fruit, snake fruit (this had a beautiful skin that looked like the scales of a snake), jackfruit, and the durian, whose powerful fetid odor I could smell from five blocks away.

Many stalls sold street food, often just cut fruit that was about to go bad. It was a great way for me to taste all these new ingredients. Each morning I tried something new. I loved that the vendors put your food in a plastic bag and you ate straight from the bag with a plastic spoon. I would arrive at the restaurant with four different kinds of breakfasts to try. I might get sticky rice with mango in one bag or a bag of pineapple and mango, with half sugar, half salt, chilies, and a wedge of lime.

I worked in the center of luxury, but the market was where the people of Thailand congregated. It was where I learned that to know a city, you should first spend time in the local markets. When you know the markets, you know the city. The food is a map of its culture, its climate, its geography, its people, its beliefs. Whenever I travel to a city I haven't been to before, the first place I go is the market. In this way, all of my food comes from memories of my travel, my food a map of where I've been.

I'd never seen people so poor. I never saw lepers in Alsace or on the French Riviera. In Bangkok, I watched one man literally fall apart during my three years there. He lost an arm. A month later, his leg was gone. Then another. By the time I left, he was nothing but a trunk on a skateboard propped against a wall.

The surrounding land, the rivers and canals and jungle, they were not clean. There were crocodiles. You'd see a dead dog floating with its bloated belly facing up, and just downstream from the dead dog, a woman would be standing in the river brushing her teeth. For me, it wasn't culture shock. It was culture electrification.

I loved it all.

In Alsace, we used a lot of spices—star anise, cardamom, cinnamon. But they didn't grow there. They came from the colonies and former colonies, and my dream had always been to go where the food was growing. I was always passionate about ginger powder—but not actual ginger. I didn't experience fresh ginger until I arrived in Thailand. Spices were dry when I was growing up. I never saw the plants, never saw fresh ginger, fresh black pepper. My goal was to travel. Geography had always been my forte in school. I loved the history, how the colonies brought different cultures and foods.

Now I was here.

Travel became my inspiration, and today it remains my greatest source of new ideas and innovation.

For nearly three years, I lived and cooked in Thailand— traveling when I was able to take a break, especially to Vietnam (I could travel there with a French passport). I bribed my way into Cambodia. I explored India. These were amazing, formative years.

And then in 1983, Outhier called. He said, "I want you to open another restaurant, in Singapore."

Lobster Thai

Bangkok was an eye-opener for Outhier. Like me, he was immediately energized by the flavors of this exotic land once called Siam—galangal, the ginger-like root with its eucalyptus scent; the many curry pastes; the fresh chilies. There was no coconut milk in France, except perhaps for the cans of sweetened stuff used for piña coladas. And as a chef, he of course wanted to start putting some of these Thai ingredients to use in his own cooking. This would be all but unheard of in France at a Michelin three-star. He was as excited as I was.

Lobster Thai was among the first Thai-inspired dishes he and I created together at the Oriental hotel in Bangkok, if not *the* first. As with all of this cooking, it's so easy you almost don't have to do anything, because the flavors are so dramatic. This is a very delicate, well-balanced curry. But there was a problem for Outhier in bringing it back home. Outhier couldn't use coconut milk at L'Oasis because he simply couldn't get it in France. He couldn't bring it back in the quantities he'd need, and shipping was nowhere near as easy as it is today. So he would have to use cream instead, slightly higher in fat and with a more neutral flavor. Outhier loved his reductions of European wines, and so for this dish he used a white port, which would contribute a similar level of sweetness and compensate for changing the coconut milk to cream.

Outhier used langouste, spiny lobster, which was available to him there. Langoustines work fine here as well, as do cold-water lobster and shrimp.

We were creating a true French-Thai fusion—I'm sure it had to be among the first of its kind, certainly at this level. When Outhier brought lobster Thai to the south of France, people were amazed. Even his hidebound three-star mafioso brothers were impressed. And Outhier was now known as the first chef to bring Asian fusion to Michelin three-star cooking.

Okay, here we go.

> 3 tablespoons unsalted butter
> ¾ teaspoon each red, yellow, and green curry
>   pastes (we use the Mae Ploy brand)
> 2 stalks lemongrass, bruised outer leaves
>   removed, cut into 4- or 5-inch pieces
> 2 to 3 Kaffir lime leaves

Put the butter and curry pastes in a pan. I use a 2-quart saucier pan, a *saucière,* really the best pan for these kinds of sauces, with its wide, sloping sides. It's my go-to pan. Sweat the paste in the butter to begin releasing the flavors. This is fairly standard in Thai cooking, sweating the paste. It's not always done there; sometimes cooks simply combine all the ingredients—liquids, aromatics, bones, meat—and bring it all to a simmer, but sweating the paste really enhances the flavor. It also smells . . . *so good* . . . while you're cooking, and you should take pleasure in this.

While the butter melts and the curry sweats, bruise the lemongrass pieces hard with the back of your knife, many times. Smell it before adding it to the pot. Crush the lime leaves between your fingers. If you're cooking with others in the kitchen, offer it to them, have them inhale the perfume. Magical. Put these in the pan as well, to get them heating and releasing their flavor, for a couple of minutes or so. I always cover the pan at this early stage—the heat and steam speeds the sweating.

1 cup julienned carrot
Salt for seasoning

Uncover the pan and add the carrots. Hit them with some salt. This will help them to begin releasing water and will soften them as they heat.

Sweat the carrots gently, stirring every so often over medium heat; they'll be releasing their own flavors and sweetness and picking up other flavors. Inhale! Chili paste, lime leaves, lemongrass. The smells are so heady, and we haven't even really done anything yet!

This is an important point: Cook the carrots till they're just past al dente. As soon as you add liquid, they'll stop cooking, so they should be tender before you add the wine.

> 2 cups white port
> 1 Golden Delicious apple (to be peeled and
>   julienned)
> 1 teaspoon turmeric

When the carrots are perfectly cooked—and you will know this by tasting them—add the port and turn the heat to high to get the wine reducing. While it's reducing, peel the apple (pole to pole, Outhier-style), and julienne it on a Benriner mandoline. Add another pinch of salt to the pan. When the port has reduced by about two-thirds, add the apple and the turmeric. When the simmer has resumed, reduce the heat a little and continue to simmer the ingredients for a few more minutes. I used the turmeric for its vibrant color and also its flavor. But it needs to cook a little or it will be gritty. Reduce the wine till it's at the level of the vegetables, has thickened to the point that the bubbles are fat and opaque, but the whole concoction remains very moist.

And you're done with the base. That's really all there is to it: sweat the vegetables, reduce the wine, and you have a fabulous base for just about any fish or chicken. You can use this base right away, or you can put it in the fridge. It will keep for two to three days. This was great for the restaurant, this base. All we're going to do to finish it is add some whipped cream and gently warm it.

2 lobsters
1 head of bok choy, about 1 pound
4 to 6 ounces unsalted butter

Before finishing this dish, you're going to have to cook the lobster and blanch and shock the bok choy. This can be done whenever you wish—before you make the curry base, while you're making it, or afterward. It's up to you. Remember, a chef's key attribute is flexibility, planning your work in accordance with your kitchen, your ingredients, and your schedule.

To cook the lobster, bring a large pot of water to a boil. Remove the tails and the arms and claws from the lobsters. (If you wish to kill the lobster first: place the tip of your chef's knife at the base of the head and press down and through the entire head; this will instantly dispatch the lobster; if you want to use a half head as a garnish, blanch and clean the heads before serving.) Put the tails and claws into the boiling water. Cook the tails for two minutes, then plunge them into an ice bath. Remove the arms and claws after four minutes (their thicker shells require a little more cooking), and plunge them into the ice bath. Halve the tails lengthwise and remove them from the shell. Remove the claw and knuckle meat from the shells. Cover and refrigerate until ready to use.

Blanche the bok choy just till tender, 30 seconds or so, then plunge it into an ice bath. Drain on paper towels and refrigerate until ready to use.

To finish the dish, preheat your oven to 350°F.

In a saucier pan, heat a couple tablespoons of

water over medium-high heat. When the water begins to simmer, add four to six ounces of butter cut into pieces, whisking continuously until the butter has melted and you have a homogeneous, pale yellow, liquefied butter (this is often referred to as *beurre monté*). Add the blanched lobster over medium heat, stirring and tossing the lobster gently in the butter. Put the lobster in the oven to heat through while you finish the dish; this should take five to ten minutes. (Once removed from the oven, the lobster can stay warm in the butter while you finish the sauce.)

1 cup whipped cream
Cilantro for garnish

When you're ready to serve the dish, fold the whipped cream into your curry base, about an equal amount of it relative to the amount of base, or a little more. Stir it over medium heat just until it simmers. Taste it and add a little more salt if it needs it. Remove it from the heat.

When the lobster is cooked—it should be hot all through but still very tender from the gentle heat of the butter (and the butter, deliciously flavored with the lobster, can be reused as you wish—try gently scrambling eggs in it), reheat the bok choy and place it in bowls. Spoon the lobster into the center of the bowls, and top with the sauce. Garnish with a rough julienne of cilantro.

SERVES 4

This is one of my very favorite dishes. The irony at the time we were developing it was that, while I had introduced Outhier to these new curries and aromatics and guided this dish into being, since I'd become so familiar with Thai cooking, I couldn't put this dish on *my* menu at Outhier's outpost. A lobster Thai curry on the menu of a French restaurant in Thailand? Are you kidding me? People would laugh. It would be a decade before I could renew the preparation for the opening of my second restaurant, Vong, in New York City.

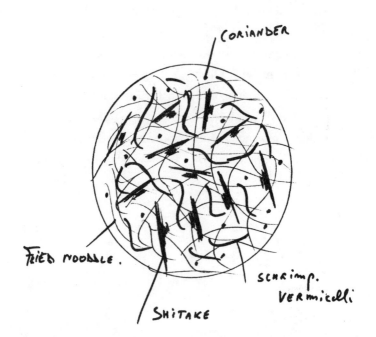

CORIANDER

FRIED NOODLE.

SHITAKE

schrimp.
VERmicelli

Interlude

ON COOKING:
THE PHILOSOPHY
OF CLEAN

WHEN A NEW COOK BEGINS TO WORK AT ONE OF MY restaurants, they learn my basics. I prefer to have somebody 100 percent green, because it's easier to teach him or her my basics. There's nothing to unlearn. Though the unlearning process happens all the time, of course—a young cook comes from a restaurant where he has learned, for instance, to peel apples in a continuous circle around the apple. I want my cooks to peel the apples in the opposite way, from pole to pole, as Outhier did. If I serve roasted duck with some Armagnac and some roasted, caramelized apples, the appearance of the apples is important. If you peel around the apple, you see ridges in the wedge of roasted apple. If you peel it my way, there are no ridges. A guy who has been peeling apples at Daniel, Daniel Boulud's Michelin-starred restaurant, for three years, he's going to start peeling my way, but as soon as I turn my back he's going to revert to the way he learned at Daniel. I've seen it a hundred times.

When you have someone green, they don't know better. I didn't know better when I started. When I began at

Auberge de l'Ill, I learned to cook in a specific way, Monsieur Paul's way, his basics. When I left, after three years, for the south of France, for L'Oasis and Chef Outhier, remember what he said to me: "Whatever you learned there, forget it. We don't cook that way."

Now I understand what he knew. So when you arrive in a new kitchen, learn those basics, consider them, adopt them, perfect them, and when you leave that kitchen, take away what makes sense to you. Because every kitchen is different and every kitchen has its own reasons for doing what it does. Even with parsley. The parsley was handled differently, and specifically, in each of my first three kitchens. To a thoughtless cook, it wouldn't make any sense. At Auberge, I was taught to cut the parsley very, very finely. At L'Oasis, I was trained always to chiffonade the parsley. Bocuse, he wanted the parsley roughly chopped. It wouldn't make sense to a cook in the back of the kitchen who didn't see how the parsley was being used. But each chef had his reasons.

Monsieur Paul used his parsley to season a Riesling sauce—he needed it finely minced for the flavor and for an elegant appearance. For Outhier, his parsley primarily served as a visual garnish, and so it had to be a beautiful chiffonade, a more time-intensive cut, done *à la minute,* of course. (In Alsace, we didn't have flat parsley, only curly, and it would have been futile to try to chiffonade it.) Bocuse loved big, bold flavors. He wanted the parsley to pop when you chewed, so he didn't want it finely chopped; nor did he need the visual appeal of the chiffonade. Again, each chef had his reasons.

*

MY NUMBER ONE RULE in all of cooking is this: Work clean. Be clean. You cook the way you look.

The first thing I teach new cooks is that before you can learn to cook in my kitchen, in any kitchen, you must learn to clean. You cannot learn to cook until you have embraced this fact, made it a part of your life. Not just in your life in the kitchen, but in your whole life. It must become not a part of the way you think, but a fundamental part of who you are.

Some people seem to be born with it, as I suspect I was, and this discipline was enforced and strengthened by my mother. Others must learn it. It's possible to learn, but learning requires diligence. I know many chefs who are not like this, chefs who don't mind if their cooks walk around with their *mise* on their shoes, and they still run successful restaurants. But I know few chefs who run top-flight restaurants who aren't fanatical about cleaning.

At many of the better sushi restaurants in Japan, when a new cook arrives, their first job is to clean the bathrooms. This sends a clear message. Thomas Keller, one of the best chefs in America, has said that when, as a teenager, he went to work as a dishwasher at the restaurant his mother managed, the first thing he had to do every day was to clean the bathrooms. "They had to *shine*," he said, because his mother was fanatical about cleaning. He wasn't even cooking yet, but when his mother tapped him to come into the kitchen, the attention to cleaning the bathrooms he'd learned served him well. So well, in fact, that after his flagship restaurant, the French Laundry, had become famous throughout the world, Keller said, "No matter what I do, it's kind of based on cleaning the bathroom."

That's how important the philosophy of clean is.

Cooking is about respect: respect for the food, respect for the people you serve, respect for yourself. And respect begins, first, not with sharp knives, not with the best ingredients, but with cleanliness. Inside and out. People who are clean, who have a clean uniform, a crisp apron, a folded side towel, a sharp knife, they are better cooks. If you see a sloppy cook—he's wiping himself everywhere, scraps cover his board, scraps are on his feet—his food will be just as sloppy. He's going to stick his finger in the sauce and lick it, twice. At Jean-Georges, I have an open kitchen where all the cooks are seen and must be impeccable. The chefs who cook for the adjoining restaurant, Nougatine, cook downstairs. No one can see them. But I want these cooks to be as clean as the cooks in the open kitchen. I want them to be ready to enter the Jean-Georges kitchen. My point is, appearances matter because they reflect what is on the inside. If you're not clean in the downstairs kitchen, how will you suddenly become clean up here? Start today—always work clean.

If you can teach somebody to be clean, they will leave as a better person and a better cook.

We have an obligation—to the food, to the customer, to our colleagues, to ourselves—to offer the best of what we are. And this begins with personal appearance.

Next comes your station. Before you can learn to cook, you must learn to clean. You and your station must be impeccable.

But how do you learn to be clean, to work clean? If you work in a place where people kick oven doors shut and twirl their tongs, that's all you know. And so you must educate yourself. Find kitchens that are immaculate and stage there. You'll know it when you see it. The cooks' uniforms and aprons will be clean throughout morning prep. The cooks will continuously be wiping down all the surfaces around them after finishing each task. The floor will be perfectly swept. When you learn to work clean, it becomes a part of you. You're clean everywhere, not just in the kitchen. It should be so much a part of you that you can't turn it on and off any more than you can change the color of your eyes.

I've been saying this for forty years. All of it works its way onto a plate. You cook the way you look—inside and out.

*

AFTER HOW TO WORK CLEAN, the second most important thing I teach new cooks about cooking is also not about cooking. It's about tasting, how to taste.

How can you cook my food without being able to evaluate it as I would evaluate it and, most importantly, adjust it? You must learn to taste as I taste. You must understand *my* seasoning. This is largely a matter of understanding the salt level, the level of acidity, the intensity of the spice or pepper, and the ideal balance between these three fundamental components. Those three components are the foundation for evaluating every dish. As cooks, we must always be tasting, so that we can adjust toward the perfect balance of those components. Even if it's a simple soup, like the tom yum kung. When it comes to adding the two most important seasoning ingredients, the fish sauce and the lime juice, I don't simply add them and that's that. I add a little less than the minimum I think I need. Then I taste and add each ingredient incrementally, tasting after each adjustment until the flavor is as close to perfect as I can make it. When seasoning a soup or stew, add salt in increments, tasting only after the salt has dissolved and been evenly distributed

But can I describe this in words, tell you what the right level of acidity is, the ideal amount of fish sauce, the balance between savory broth and lime juice? No. When you work in my kitchen, I taste, then you taste. That's the only way my taste can become your taste.

*

SHARP KNIVES—I shouldn't need to say this, but I do—are essential. We teach all our cooks how to sharpen their knives on a Japanese stone. Japanese cooks are, as a rule, very good sharpeners; they don't go home until their knives are ready for the next day's work. You can't rely on someone else to sharpen your knives. Learn to do it yourself, carry your stone with you, and you will always have sharp edges.

You can't cut properly without a sharp knife. Your cuts will be inaccurate. There is no way to achieve precise and uniform cuts in a small dice or brunoise if you don't have a sharp knife. You have to push too hard to get a dull blade through the food. Herbs need to be sliced; you can't slice delicate herbs with a dull knife.

The surprising fact is that not enough people realize

that food cut with a sharp knife actually *tastes* better than food cut with a dull knife—a dull knife smashes through food rather then slices, damaging cell walls, affecting both flavor and texture. The quality of knives today is remarkable, so much better than when I began. It's up to you to keep them sharp.

*

WE MEASURE JUST ABOUT everything other than the salt we season our meat or fish with. Measuring is the best way to ensure consistency across the board. I learned this in pastry at Auberge de l'Ill, and its importance has never diminished in my mind. I have 16 restaurants in New York City, 20 more throughout the world. I can't be at them all, tasting and adjusting. Even when I'm *at* Jean-Georges, the restaurant where I spend most of my time, the food can't be 100 percent me.

I do the food—it's my passion, my flavor—but if I pass it to the guy next to me, the dish loses a little bit of my particular style. Something of me that's in the recipe gets lost. It's kind of like the game telephone: one person tells a story to the next, and ten people later it's a completely different story. Same thing with food: the farther the recipe gets from the chef, the more the food varies from the original.

If you're cooking for yourself or for a small group, you cook, you season to taste, you serve. It's 100 percent you. But as soon as you work as a team, whether it's six cooks or twenty or fifty cooks, you have to give up part of yourself. You're going to lose 20 percent. Because every cook has a different touch, a different palate, no matter the kitchen. My vision is not necessarily the same as that of the guy on the fish station. When you eat at one of my restaurants, or one of Daniel Boulud's restaurants, or Tom Colicchio's, you're inevitably missing a part of the chef who imagined the food. And my fight every day is to close that gap. To make it 18 percent, 15 percent. It's frustrating for a chef, and it is the reason chefs can find learning to delegate so difficult. And yet delegating is inevitable if you're going to grow.

One way I try to close the gap is by relying on precise recipes for consistency. All my kitchens use scales, and all ingredients are measured to the gram.

*

THE INTERNET AND GOOGLE—these didn't exist when I was a young chef. I had only my kitchen and the local library for information. Google is a miracle of information. If I wanted to learn about tamarind when I was first making my way as a cook, I'd have to travel to a library and hunt through a card catalog and locate a book. If you want to know about tamarind—*click*—and in moments you know nearly everything there is to know about it: where it grows, what it looks like on the tree, when it's harvested, the different types, and how to process it. In an instant, twenty thousand recipes that use it are at your disposal. I had to travel to learn how to smash lemongrass. Today, you click and there's a video demonstration. Google is a new kind of mentor, scary but awesome. Yet despite this bounty, you should always keep in mind the source of the information you're receiving. Be skeptical. Because you read it on the Internet doesn't make it true.

Google cannot teach you what tamarind actually tastes

like, or the way it affects food when you cook with it, or how its acidity differs from that of lemon juice. Google cannot teach you to take pleasure in the aroma of the lemongrass that you now know how to smash properly. Google can't teach you how to be more efficient on the line, how to develop speed, how to refine your palate, how to inspire a team, or how to please many different kinds of people with your food.

The Internet is an extraordinary tool, but you must also be aware of its limitations.

*

A LA MINUTE COOKING, cooking by sight and smell and touch, is inevitably imprecise, but for the restaurant we try to be as precise as possible. Seasoning meat and fish we do by sight as well. In these cases we don't measure, so this cooking must be learned through repetition.

Seasoning—or, more precisely, salting—is another of the basics that must be learned. Salt, of course, as far as basic ingredients go, is paramount. It is perhaps the most important ingredient in the kitchen. And because we salt many items by hand, learning how much salt you pick up between your fingers, how much salt you rain on the food is critical.

When we make a sauce like the caper-raisin emulsion, we weigh the salt along with the other ingredients. But when we season a piece of fish or a piece of meat we're about to sauté, we don't weigh the salt. And seasoning a thick piece of meat is different from seasoning a thin piece of turbot. We must teach new cooks how we season, and new cooks must be observant and must learn the nuances of seasoning. Seasoning spinach, for instance—spinach has so much salt in it that you barely need any salt, so often it's overseasoned.

In France, we use fine sea salt for basic seasoning. When I arrived in the United States, where coarse kosher salt is used, I had to learn how to salt food all over again, because the amounts I picked up between my fingers was different. The finer the grain, the more salt by weight you pick up. So I was underseasoning everything for weeks. And whenever I go back to France and use the fine salt, I overseason everything!

Of course, salt comes in many forms. Notice that when I'm making the tom yum kung, I don't think to myself, "Now I add the fish sauce"; rather I think, "Now I add my salt, fish sauce." Cooks in Japan use very little sea salt or kosher salt—instead they rely on soy sauce for their salt, as well as the saltiness of seaweed.

I love the crystalline salts, fleur de sel and Maldon salt, for their crunch. But those are for finishing dishes, not all-purpose seasoning salts.

Acidity follows salt in order of importance. And you must attain just the right balance. The heavy, rich foods of Alsace needed lots of acidity. And so I bring that awareness of acidity to most of the food I cook. Again, look at the tom yum kung. There are so many lessons in that soup. You salt it with the fish sauce, you season it with lime, and with just those two ingredients, and the aromatics of the lemongrass and the lime leaves, water becomes a light, delicious broth. But put too much lime in and the soup turns sour.

The same rules apply to sauces in terms of seasoning,

acidity, and spice. Chef Outhier was the best saucier. He loved to work the fish station—fish were his passion. I learned the sauces from him, mainly by watching how he did the *vin blanc*, the fumet, watching and tasting. He was all about salt, pepper or cayenne, and acidity. The butter and wine sauces for fish especially need aggressive acidity.

As a rule: *I want all my sauces to be three times as powerful as the meat or the fish they are served with.*

That's the kind of force a sauce must have; otherwise you won't taste it and the dish will lack contrast. *Three times as powerful.* Hollandaise has to be really, really lemony, three times as powerful as the sole, the turbot it goes with.

It's only after such basics are mastered that a young cook can begin to learn the nuances of cooking specific ingredients, how to best handle them. For instance, halibut is best cooked in plentiful butter, rolled and basted. The fat draws out the excess fish oils, and the low temperature of the butter can't overheat those oils, so that the fish tastes very fresh and clean. Overheated fish oils are often responsible for an unpleasantly fishy taste. One of my favorite ways of cooking salmon is to roast it in a low oven, so low that the oils the heat releases aren't overcooked. Ten minutes in a 250°F oven is all you need. You're basically just warming it.

Cooking daily and paying attention, you gradually develop the knowledge of individual items, such as the halibut and the salmon. You learn that white asparagus, for instance, needs to be peeled twice or the stalks will taste woody, and that they must be cooked until completely tender, not al dente like green asparagus.

How does one properly reduce a bottle of wine? Chef Outhier often used a vermouth reduction. But he didn't simply pour a bottle of wine into a pan and boil away. He always reduced wine in three steps. Pour a third of the bottle into a small pan over medium-low heat and reduce it by half. Add another third and again reduce by half, then add the last third and reduce to the desired consistency and strength. If you reduce the wine all at once, or even in two additions, the flavor will be overcaramelized. Wine reduced incrementally tastes powerfully of the wine, with a clean, concentrated wine flavor. Once, when the chef left the restaurant and I was behind schedule, I poured a whole bottle into the pan and let it reduce while I returned to my cutting board. But when Outhier came back and tasted my reduction, he squinted, shook his head, and said, "Something's not right. You reduced this all at once." I had to admit that I had. And Outhier was absolutely right. A wine reduced incrementally has a depth and clarity that a quickly reduced wine lacks.

The level of the flame below your pan is also critical. I see so many cooks put a small saucepan on a burner and crank it to high without thinking. Often, the flames reach up the sides of the pan. Your flame should be below the pan, not scorching the sides. This drives me crazy, in large part because it tells me the cook isn't thinking, but is instead simply turning the heat as high as it will go.

Cooking is infinitely nuanced. One learns a thousand small points, such as how to properly reduce wine or heat your pan. No Internet search can give you all of this, and no book or library can, either. But we can describe the essence of cooking. This is relatively simple: work clean, keep your knives sharp, measure carefully, pay attention to salt and acid, develop a sense of taste. The rest of cooking follows from these fundamentals.

And there may be no more valuable attribute than your own intrinsic curiosity, curiosity about all things, and the ability to watch, to pay attention, to see what goes on in the kitchen.

BECOMING
A CHEF

PART IV

Our 1987 Christmas card features so many wonderful chefs: Lois Freedman (first row third from left), Ron Gallo (same row far right), and Pierre Schutz (back row far right) are all still with me.

10.

LEAVE NOTHING
TO CHANCE

IN 1983, MOVING AT FULL THROTTLE AT THE ORIENTAL hotel in Bangkok, I got the call from Outhier. He'd been contacted by executives at the Méridien hotel in Singapore. They'd asked him to open a restaurant there, and he wanted me to be the one to make that happen. I would need to prepare to leave the Bangkok restaurant to open in Singapore. I didn't want to leave—I'd just begun to learn this place, and I loved it. I lived like a king. But I had no choice. Outhier needed me.

*

ARRIVING IN SINGAPORE, having lived three years in Thailand, was like arriving in Switzerland. It was so clean. It had been founded as a British colony in the early 1800s and had only recently, in the 1960s, gained its independence, first from Britain and then from Malaysia. So it was a young and sterile place when I showed up, and it still felt solidly colonial. There were no opium dens here. You weren't even allowed to chew gum in public.

This new land stood in stark contrast to the wildness of

Bangkok, but it also had an amazingly diverse conglomeration of cultures, with large immigrant populations from India, China, Malaysia, Indonesia, the Philippines, and elsewhere. So it was also a melting pot of all the best cuisines of Southeast Asia. The best Malaysian food, the best Indonesian, the best Chinese, the best Muslim vegetarian cuisine. By going to this specific and unusual territory, Singapore, I got an education in four or five cuisines. Again my imagination expanded and expanded again as I learned these new cuisines and saw all the new ingredients and styles and techniques.

Opening in Singapore was easier than opening in Bangkok. The country was more organized, and this time, I knew what I was doing. Outhier found that this business model worked beautifully, so within seven months, I found myself packing up my family again to move to Hong Kong, to open there for Outhier. And then soon we were traveling again, relocating in Osaka, Japan.

I spent three years opening and then working at the Oriental in Bangkok. And then I spent the next three years opening *seven* more restaurants. From Japan, I moved to Geneva; then we opened in Lisbon, and then in London. At last Outhier sent me to the United States, to Boston, to open a restaurant in the Hotel Lafayette (now the Hyatt Regency).

The Lafayette was in what was then a seedy part of town, called the Combat Zone, right on the edge of Chinatown. But it was an elegant hotel. I was happy to be there and excited to be in the United States for the first time. There were some good chefs in Boston at the time—Lydia Shire, Jasper White, Frank McClelland. And I loved

Boston. Until I visited New York, that is—I knew almost immediately that Manhattan was where I was meant to be.

I went to the Fulton Fish Market, walked Chinatown, got my first taste of the explosive restaurant scene, and I thought, "What am I doing in Boston? New York is the place. I've got to get myself to New York."

That was exactly what I set out to do. I didn't leave it to chance.

The mid-1980s in Manhattan were seminal years in the history of restaurants, with an influence not just in America but worldwide. You could feel it. The city had an amazing vibe. Daniel Boulud led the kitchen at the Polo Lounge. Thomas Keller was one of his chefs. David Bouley had teamed up with Drew Nieporent to create Montrachet, a kitchen that launched many chefs' careers. Larry Forgione explored American cuisine at An American Place. Brendan Walsh's Arizona 206 covered southwestern American cuisine. Patrick Clark had made the Odeon a downtown destination. Alfred Portale took the helm of Gotham Bar and Grill, where such future luminaries as Bill Telepan, Scott Bryan, and Tom Valenti would cook. David Burke and the restaurateur Danny Meyer, both in their twenties, appeared on the scene. And just as I arrived, Gilbert and Maguy Le Coze opened Le Bernardin.

New York City was a hotbed of talent, and I was eager to relocate there. We would all be watching one another, seeing what others were cooking, pushing and being pushed by one another. Old-school French restaurants, which had once held sway over the city, were about to be eclipsed by this new talent. It was a lucky time, and place, to be a chef, with America on the edge of a culinary revolution.

Right away, the *Boston Globe* gave the restaurant I'd opened, Le Marquis de Lafayette, four stars, but some of the thrill was lost on me, because by then I could do Outhier's food with my eyes closed. Salmon mousse and crayfish served on a bed of leeks, saddle of lamb with a potato crust, John Dory on a *beurre blanc,* foie gras in almond pastry.

The Hotel Lafayette was owned by the Swissôtel group, along with its sister hotel in New York, the Drake. I stayed there when I went to the city. After my first visits, I had a talk with the hotel's general manager. I told him what we were doing in Boston, showed him the rave reviews, and said, "We could do the same thing right here in New York." The Drake Hotel already had its own restaurant, the Café Suisse, which served bistro fare, schnitzel and *bündnerfleisch.* But this elegant hotel, I argued, should have a first-class restaurant.

I had thus planted the seed of the idea in the mind of the GM. In other words, sometimes you can't just wait for things to go your way. On a subsequent visit, after some poking around, I discovered that the lease for the shoe store adjoining the hotel was nearly up. I made sure the general manager was aware of this. We could take it over and do a proper restaurant, I suggested. Sure enough, the corporate office of Swissôtel contacted Outhier about opening at the Drake Hotel, on Manhattan's Park Avenue. And soon I was on my way to New York.

But it wasn't going to be easy. The suits who ran the hotel intended to create a 120-seat restaurant and have me share the kitchen with the Café Suisse, the restaurant that serviced the hotel—breakfast, lunch, dinner, and room service. The executives asked me what I thought. I told them it wouldn't work. I couldn't do Outhier's food from the same kitchen that was cranking out scrambled eggs and schnitzel. If they wanted a world-class French restaurant, the sort I'd opened from Bangkok to Boston, they were going to have to build a new kitchen.

They said there was no room for a kitchen. I told them to put it *in* the restaurant. We should have an open kitchen, I argued, and eighty seats, not 120. The manager and others at the hotel thought I was crazy, but Outhier and I convinced them, and once they were on board, everything was done right. I was still working in Boston, so the architect faxed me daily. I just had to say, "I need six burners here, six burners there, two ovens here, a *plancha* here, two salamanders here." In the end, they built a beautiful kitchen, with all new equipment, gleaming copper pans, silver cloches.

It would be one of New York City's first show kitchens, if not the first. Wolfgang Puck had opened his first restaurant, Spago, a few years earlier; it had an open kitchen, but it was an L.A.-casual restaurant serving pizzas. New York didn't yet have any establishment with an open kitchen, and in high-end French restaurants this arrangement was unheard of anywhere in the United States.

I hadn't asked for this open format casually. It was part of my plan to make a new restaurant in a form that meshed with where I saw American cuisine was now but then built on that, toward where it was heading. Chefs like Boulud and Keller were capturing New York's attention. I wanted my chefs onstage. I wanted the action of the kitchen to be a *part* of the dining experience—and the diners, I knew, would enjoy this, too. I wanted my chefs to be on view and to *know* they were being watched, and watched with great interest, because their work was fascinating and important. This would make my chefs strive to up their game. And I thought it would be synergistic for them to be able to see the customer responding to their food. Before then, they were cut off from the people they were serving. No longer.

Chefs need to think about the entire room, not just the menu and the kitchen; they need to consider the whole experience of the restaurant.

I was determined to make Restaurant Lafayette, in the Drake Hotel, an exciting new restaurant in the most dynamic city in the world. I would move my wife and children—we'd had a second child, a daughter, Louise—to the Drake less than a year after arriving in Boston. But I wanted to stay classical—true to Outhier. This was my eighth Outhier opening. Don't fix it if it isn't broken, I thought. Diners today are so much more open to chefs' ideas today, to *omakase* menus. But at the time, 1986, they had specific expectations of a French restaurant. We offered a straightforward menu: eight appetizers, eight mains, and a tasting menu. And it worked well, though I was now in New York City, and this city had unspoken rules I had to learn.

11.

LESSONS FROM FISH

NEW YORK IS THE TOUGHEST RESTAURANT CITY IN THE world, the toughest audience to please. And the toughest place to do business.

From the beginning, I had a hard time getting fish into my New York City kitchen—or, rather, getting good, fresh fish. The hotel bought from a big purveyor. I'll call it the Stinky Fish Co. Stinky Fish bought from big fishing boats that would be out on the ocean for a week, then bring the fish in, scale them, bone them, and let them marinate in the fridge for a few more days; only then would they sell the fish to you. I grew very depressed about my fish.

My first savior in the seafood department had appeared a year earlier, at my Boston restaurant. I'll never forget it. A server brought back a plate from a customer. The customer had said she wouldn't eat the fish because clearly it had been on ice for three or four days. I thought, "Who the hell is this?" I went to the table to meet the woman, Ingrid Bengis. She was from Stonington, Maine. She repeated her contention that the halibut wasn't fresh. Okay, she was right, I told her; it had been on ice exactly that amount of time, but it was still good halibut. She then told me her entire life story. She had been a controversial author in the 1970s and had retreated to rural Maine to get away from the notoriety. She began selling mushrooms that grew in her area to Balducci's. Then she began to explore what other products could be found in her ecologically pristine coast. She told me she would show me what good halibut was.

Two days later, a big box arrived. It was filled with seaweed and the biggest halibut I'd ever seen. The whole thing, head and all—I'd never seen a halibut with its head on. When I'd opened the box, a wave of cucumber had wafted out. The fish was so fresh it smelled of cucumber. It was so big I could barely fillet it. I immediately cut a piece off and cooked it. Five minutes later, I had her on the phone and was placing my first order. I would soon be receiving her crab, scallops, and lobsters as well. And Ingrid, who was just starting out, would go on to sell to all the top restaurants in the country: Le Bernardin, the French Laundry, everyone. You had to use her product well, or she wouldn't sell to you. You had to earn her business. She was something else.

One of the great things about Ingrid was how she cared about the fishermen in her state. What they did, how hard the work was, why their fish was so amazing. For the first time in a dozen years, I was getting a real education in fish. She was the reason I understood how bad the fish from the Stinky Fish Company was. She was an educator as well as a purveyor. A wonderful woman. I worked with her for thirty-three years, until her death in 2017.

She was the first person to teach me about the kind of fish I could find in America.

Then, not long after I moved to New York and opened Lafayette there, I met Gilbert Le Coze. Gilbert had had a seafood restaurant in Paris but had closed it down so that he and his sister, Maguy, could focus on their New York outpost of Le Bernardin, the best seafood restaurant in New York, in the country. Gilbert knew his fish. Also, he spoke French, which was a great help to me. I'd begun taking English lessons back in Bangkok, but my English still wasn't great, even after a year in the States. So my first friends in New York were French speakers, Gilbert and the American chef David Bouley. It was Gilbert who took me to the fish market, showed me where the best fish purveyors were. He introduced me to the smaller fishermen who ran day boats. And he helped educate me about fish. Being from Alsace, I had developed expertise in freshwater fish—trout, pike, eel. Gilbert helped further my education in saltwater fish—John Dory, Atlantic black sea bass, dorade.

The problem was, none of the main vendors at the fish market would sell to me, because they knew where I worked and they knew that the Drake Hotel was a customer of the Stinky Fish Co. These vendors didn't want pushback from this player.

Week after week, no matter how much I complained and begged for fresher fish, I got sent stinky cod, stinky skate, stinky monkfish. So I took the fish we were getting to the general manager of Lafayette and Café Suisse. It was obvious even to him that this was poor-quality fish. He told me to go to the market and find the smaller fishermen Gilbert had introduced me to, who would sell to me; their boats left the dock at five a.m. and returned at noon with what they had caught. So I began going to the market, and at last, after nearly six months of having to use the Stinky Fish Co. exclusively, I could finally get pristine seafood.

One morning before I headed to the Fulton Fish Market, the night manager told me that I could take his car to the market if I brought him back a couple of sea bass. I thought, "Sure—much faster and easier." And it was a great car, a big-ass Cadillac. I parked it at the market and went to do my buying. An hour later, I returned with my fish to find the Cadillac up on blocks, all four tires gone.

I don't know who did this for certain, but I figured it had to be the work of Stinky Fish. That's New York. I took a taxi back to the hotel, with my fish and the night manager's sea bass. I told him where his car was and that I'd pay for the tires.

But I was happy. It was worth the cost. From then on, I could buy from any purveyor I wanted. I was developing relationships with all the best possible purveyors.

In this way, I was learning that a chef must develop solid relationships with his or her purveyors and farmers—and have an understanding and appreciation of their work. If you're not good to your purveyors or your farmers and, even more important, appreciate what they are up against—the weather, the seasons, and the many facets of their world—and if you don't recognize that you need to be flexible, they're not going to bring you the best ingredients. If you're miserable with everybody, it's going to show on your plate. All this I was learning.

Everything was falling into place in New York. The glowing reviews came pouring in, as ever. I could do no wrong. I had opened in seven cities in six years, all of them to the highest acclaim. I was in the most exciting city in the world, one filled with chefs who were about to burst onto the international scene. And I was ready to join them. I was at the top of my game.

Then Gael Greene came to eat.

Me and my dashing mentor, Louis Outhier.

12.

LISTEN TO CRITICS

YOU MUST HAVE A RELATIONSHIP WITH YOUR CUSTOM-ers in order to get better. You must be open to what they say. If you cook only what you like but nobody else likes it, you will fail, no matter what you do. Half of what I do in my kitchens comes from my customers.

When I began in kitchens and through the 1980s, chefs did not have to deal directly with the customers, or with anyone other than the cooks. They were back in the kitchen, behind closed doors, out of sight. The maître d' was the face and voice of the restaurant. Subsequently, the chef could be tough, dictatorial, angry, even abusive. Chefs then had little contact with the people eating their food. And they certainly didn't have to *listen* to customers.

But in the 1990s, the media set chefs center stage in the drama of the American food revolution. We opened the kitchens to the customers. We put chefs on television and in the movies. Publishers hungered for their cookbooks. Subsequently, chefs had to start listening to their custom-ers, working with people. We had to begin to articulate a philosophy and be accessible to the media.

Likewise, criticism of chefs changed dramatically. In the 1980s, when I first began cooking in New York, there was Gael Greene, restaurant critic for *New York* magazine, and Bryan Miller, restaurant critic for the *New York Times*. That was pretty much it. There was no Internet. No Yelp. No pictures spread via smartphones. You could know a restaurant by only going to it or by reading about it. And Gael and Bryan were the most powerful voices in the city. Everyone who cared about restaurants read them every week. Critics were professional customers.

*

I'M NOT SURE THAT in 1986, when I opened Restaurant Lafayette in the Drake Hotel, anyone quite realized that American restaurants were on the cusp of enormous change. In New York, I did what I'd been doing for the past six years—spent eighteen hours a day in the restaurant. But I didn't walk through a food market, past fermenting fish and lepers, as I had in Bangkok. Here, at the end of the day, I took an elevator up to my apartment in the hotel, showered, and fell asleep in front of the television. Because I'd been doing the same thing in new cities, I loved my work. I never got bored, and I never got tired of it, because I was always traveling. Restaurant life was exciting.

New York was a thrilling city to open in. The hotel owners had built a dazzling restaurant and a perfect kitchen, with hanging copper pots that twinkled in the bright kitchen lights. The dining room was hushed, muted with low lights, the walls a beige cream color, with dark leather banquettes along one wall. The food was all Outhier. I continued to serve his classic dishes, such as the scrambled eggs with caviar and cream. I found great game right away and served venison, pheasant, and rabbit dishes. And, of course, foie gras, both sautéed on wild mushrooms and a foie gras terrine with a crunchy almond crust. Desserts were likewise refined, classic but inventive, everything from a chestnut-whiskey mousse cake to a bright and brilliant raspberry tart.

We immediately got raves. In October 1986, three months after we opened, Bryan Miller gave us three stars and a glowing review. "Just when I was becoming cynical about all these famous jet-set chefs who lend their names to restaurants and swoop into town periodically to help out the presumably inadequate kitchen staff, along comes Louis Outhier," he began, concluding that Lafayette was "one of the most significant restaurants" to open in New York City that year.

And I remembered that review especially—because of my dishwasher.

My dishwasher—I'll call him Sam—had been working at the hotel for twenty years, and he took his midday break from twelve to twelve forty-five. We got kind of busy at lunchtime, as you can imagine. Lunch service is fast, maybe more intense than dinner, because it's not spread over a long evening but spans only two, two and a half hours. New Yorkers want to get in and get out, all of them at the same time. Still, Sam, my dish man, vanished in the middle of the busiest time of the day, every day.

I said, "Sam, please, could you take your break at eleven? Or after lunch service?" He said no. It was driving me crazy, because in the middle of service, the cooks would have to wash their own pots. *I* was back there washing pots. And then one lunch service Bryan Miller came in. It was his third visit, so we knew we were being reviewed. We had one hundred covers that day. I pleaded with Sam to stay. "Sam, I'm begging you," I said. "Just today, please stay. I'll give you fifty dollars if you'll stay."

"Sorry," he said. And he left.

I needed him so badly, I'd offered to pay him out of my own pocket. How could I do my job this way? He didn't give a damn. He was union. He knew I couldn't do a thing. And I knew it, too.

I was furious. Normally, when everybody's doing their job, I'm an easygoing guy, but this I couldn't take. I would be in the back washing dishes when I needed to be concentrating on the *New York Times*' restaurant critic's food! We got the meal done, we got through service, but I was waiting for Sam to return. This couldn't continue.

He came back late, as if to rub it in. I whispered to my chef de cuisine, "Pierre, when the restaurant empties out, I'm going to talk to the guy. Stand by the walk-in. I need to have a word with Sam."

After the restaurant had cleared out, I called Sam into the walk-in. Pierre saw us enter and stood in front of the door so no one would enter. I immediately started yelling at Sam, and Sam yelled back. He got overheated. I got overheated. I couldn't help myself. I punched him. I kicked him. I'm not proud of it, but I beat the shit out of him. In the walk-in. People could hear—and no one did anything. I took out months of anger on this guy. Pierre was holding the door shut. So many months of stifling my anger—I exploded. I'm not proud of it; it's just what happened.

We left the walk-in, and Sam ran to security. I was scared. What, I wondered, was going to happen? I could get fired. But when Sam returned, Pierre asked him, "What did you do, did you fall down the stairs?" Nobody else said anything. There were no witnesses. Sam didn't have any proof. The whole kitchen staff knew that I hated the guy. Security talked to Pierre, but he said, "I don't know what happened." Everyone in the kitchen knew what had happened, and nobody said a word.

Still, I thought I was going to get fired. I had just started here, had been in New York for mere months. I hid in my office. I heard I'd broken the guy's nose.

I stayed gone for the rest of the day. When I finally got the courage to return to the kitchen the following morning, everyone clapped! I saw a new dishwasher in Sam's place. Sam had been transferred. Nothing happened to me, except that I got a dishwasher who worked during lunch. I had never punched *anybody* in my life before. I never fought.

I don't recommend violence as a rule, but I felt that I had to protect my restaurant, and my staff, from someone who was hurting it.

And you know what? Sam and I eventually made up. We're friends to this day. As I said earlier, always leave on good terms.

*

THAT SAME FALL, another critic came in. The December 1986 issue of *New York* magazine appeared, and all the fanfare I'd enjoyed suddenly meant nothing.

Gael Greene reviewed a series of restaurants in a long

article that concluded with an evaluation of Lafayette. The food merited three paragraphs, in which she called my salmon mille-feuille a "flub," my John Dory rubbery, and said that the skate left an unpleasant aftertaste—thanks, no doubt, to the Stinky Fish Co. The venison was vapid, she said, and the blueberry sauce I'd paired with it was too sweet. Scarcely a single dessert impressed her. She noted that many critics had gone "gaga" over Lafayette, but not her. She concluded the review by saying that she didn't care if she ever came back.

Because this was before chefs were the focus of criticism and praise, I wasn't even mentioned by name. Lafayette, Greene wrote, had opened "with three-star chef Louis Outhier flown in from his L'Oasis, on the Côte d'Azur, to create the menu." The review was all about the menu, not about me. But now I felt beat up. Although it was Outhier's style, it was my food, too, food I was personally making and sending to our customers. I took it personally. I was twenty-nine, and I thought, "Who *is* this person?" Only I didn't think the word "person," I was so furious. She was saying we were just another French restaurant cooking with cream and butter, and who needs it?

The bottom line is that I care what people think; I care what critics think. Deeply. And you should, too. The food I send out is my work, is me. And this woman hated it.

I took to my bed and I slept it off. Sometimes that's all you can do. If you get a bad review, sleep it off and get up ready to go back to work in the morning. I think that one took me three days in bed, but I slept it off. I had to admit that this experienced critic couldn't be 100 percent wrong. I had to evaluate what she'd written and think about it.

I had a talk with my general manager, Tony Fortuna, a great guy and an elegant front-of-the-house man. He said, "The food is okay, but we're not going to fill the place, not like this." He and I agreed that we had to lighten everything, food and service and time.

Then I called Outhier. I translated the review to him. We talked. I thought, "How could we be so off? What did customers really *want*?"

"Chef," I said, "we've got to change."

Shellfish in Spiced Carrot Broth

I was still smarting as 1986 drew to a close, after Gael Greene had basically raked me over the coals. Although I hadn't been named personally in her article, it was my work that she had found so disappointing, and I took her criticism very personally. After I recovered from that blow, I knew I had to change. New Yorkers were tired of heavy French food. But that was what I knew. Still, New Yorkers were always in a hurry. I understood. I watched them, observed them.

At the time, I was in the habit of drinking a glass of carrot juice every morning. It was delicious and refreshing. I thought, "Why don't I use this as a sauce base instead of a stock or a fumet?" It worked, and my career pivoted on that spot. I first went back to my memories of Alsace to refamiliarize myself with the seasoning, and I used carrot cake as my profile, infusing it with sweet spices. But then I thought, "Why not infuse it with the Thai aromatics I love so much, lime leaves and lemongrass and lime juice and fish sauce?"

And I first served the sauce with shrimp, which is how I'll present it here. But it is also fabulous with lobster. Or it could be a great base for a variety of shellfish, a kind of Thai bouillabaisse.

A whole new style evolved for me from this one revelation. I went crazy with the juices. I paired scallops with zucchini juice; I paired celery juice with Roquefort cheese for a saddle of veal. We revised and reorganized the entire menu, not by appetizers and entrées but, rather, by the new categories I was cooking in: broths, vinaigrettes, oils, and juices.

Forced by criticism into thinking anew, I combined creativity (using the carrot juice in a new way, revolutionary for its time) with knowledge few of my contemporaries had at the time (a deep immersion in the flavors of Southeast Asia); I took this creativity and knowledge and applied my long training in classical French techniques to come up with one new dish, and then I applied this idea to a broader strategy for cooking in general that I knew New Yorkers would embrace. They loved the new food, and many diners would come back simply to see what I had come up with next. They made me push myself to find more and more uncommon combinations. Because of this, I always say thank you to Gael.

This dish is such a simple one, but it's so powerful and good. This and my entire new way of cooking is collected in my first book, *Simple Cuisine,* but here I want to walk you through the exact way I cooked it at Lafayette. It remains a dish I'm proud of, one that is so meaningful to me personally. In many ways, I live through the food I cook.

Here I love the way the sweetness of the sauce matches the sweetness of the shellfish; I love the combination of earth and sea and the heat from the Thai chilies. If you want to make the entrée more substantial, you can set the shrimp on a mixture of cooked grains, such as barley, wheat berries, quinoa, wild rice, millet, and so on, as we sometimes did at the restaurant.

Oddly, the hardest part about serving this dish to New Yorkers was getting them to use a spoon with a main course. It's funny, I know, but we had to instruct the diners to cut the seafood and then use a spoon to scoop it up with a big mouthful of sauce.

This was a whole new me—my separation from Outhier and French cuisine. I didn't abandon French techniques (I still mounted the carrot juice with plenty of butter!), but I moved into a new way of thinking.

In a saucepan over medium heat, combine all the sauce ingredients:

2½ cups carrot juice
2 tablespoons finely chopped lemongrass
1 Kaffir lime leaf, finely chopped
1 or 2 Thai chilies, finely chopped
4 tablespoons lime juice
Salt to taste

Bring the juice up to heat just before a simmer to allow the aromatics and the chilies to infuse it and cook for about ten minutes. Don't bring it to a boil or it may separate. Take time to smell the broth as it infuses—these are the smells of Southeast Asia. Add a hit of salt. Taste and add more lime juice if necessary.

While the sauce is infusing, prepare the garnish.

2 to 4 tablespoons unsalted butter
2 cups small diced carrots, blanched just until
  al dente
Salt to taste

Combine these ingredients in a sauté pan over medium heat and cook until everything is just heated through. Season with salt to taste.

4 tablespoons unsalted butter

When the garnish is ready, turn up the heat on the sauce and *monté au beurre*—that is, whisk in the butter. Taste it one last time to make sure you have enough acidity and salt. Always feel free to mount more butter into the sauce.

1½ pounds large shrimp (under 16 count)
Grapeseed oil as needed for sautéing

Sauté the shrimp, just until done, a minute or two per side or a minute on one side, then flip and finish in a hot oven while you ready the bowls.

Arrange the cooked shrimp in bowls and spoon the sauce and carrots over the shrimp.

1 tablespoon mint chiffonade
1 tablespoon cilantro chiffonade

Sprinkle the herbs over the shrimp and serve immediately. Remember to use a spoon!

SERVES 4

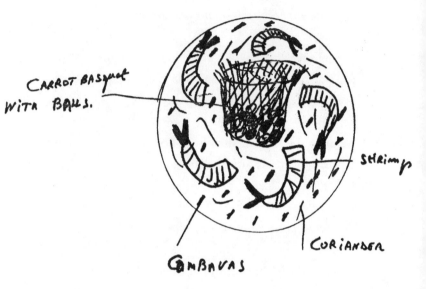

CARROT BASKET
WITH BALLS.

SHRIMP

COMBAVAS

CORIANDER

The original dish of shrimp in carrot juice, with
cilantro, lime leaves, and, in the center, a basket made
of fried carrot containing tender carrot balls.

13.

PUT FLAVOR FIRST

IN NEW YORK, I WAS LEARNING THE IMPORTANCE OF NOT only listening to my customers, but watching them, paying attention to what their actions could tell me. Praise and adoration are great, but they don't teach you anything. And if that's all you're in this for, you're in the wrong business.

I could see that New Yorkers were impatient, always in a hurry. They didn't want to sit for a three-hour lunch. This wasn't France, where that kind of lunch was de rigueur. I had to speed the meal up, keep the courses coming. I had to adjust my pace to match that of my customers.

The second thing I noticed was that diners were beginning to resist traditional French preparations, with their reliance on butter and cream. New Yorkers wanted elegance and refinement, but they didn't want all that fat.

That's when I came up with carrot juice sauce—then seasoned with allspice, cinnamon, and cayenne, with some lemon juice for acidity and (just a little) butter for richness and texture.

We tried it out on the lunch menu as a sauce for steamed shrimp, and it was a hit.

I continued to work on the sauce. I added more spices—star anise, cloves—but then I thought, "Wait, what about lime leaves and lemongrass, which have practically become part of the fiber of my being? And fresh chilies!" I added these. To make the sauce super-elegant, I decided to serve it with lobster. People taste lemongrass in carrot juice, and they think, "Amazing!" So now we had carrot juice seasoned with dry spices, infused with the Thai aromatics, and finished with butter and lime juice and Thai chilies.

It was the best sauce ever. People loved it. They would come back and say, "What do you have this week?" I had to invent some new dishes.

Almost no fine-dining restaurants in New York were cooking with chilies and lemongrass and ginger in 1987. Certainly no French restaurants were. But the people were ready for a new cuisine.

Outhier visited and began tasting some of these dishes. He said, "Trust your instincts. You're on fire."

And so I went with my instincts. I got rid of the heavy stock-based sauces and moved to lighter broths. I would infuse a vegetable broth with ginger and then, instead of enriching it with butter, I would mount foie gras fat into it and serve it with sautéed foie gras and caramelized mango.

I believed that people wanted simple foods for lunch, like roast chicken, so I installed a rotisserie in our kitchen.

Instead of serving meat and fish with rich cream sauces, I paired them with vinaigrettes—a soy-ginger vinaigrette, a juniper vinaigrette. I began to infuse oils with mustard seed, with fennel, with leek, with ginger. I would do seared scallops not in the French coquilles Saint Jacques style, with a cream sauce, but, instead, seared and served with segments of lime and a curry oil. Or I would keep it Mediterranean and poach the scallops in zucchini broth. (I should note that poaching in vegetable juice was not a new idea. One of my favorite cookbooks when I was young was Ali-Bab's *Gastronomie pratique,* published in 1907. Ali-Bab created vegetable "waters" to use as a cooking medium some eighty years before I took up the style. All culinary innovations are relative to their time.)

I had extraordinary success marrying East and West, typically using a bridging device. That is, I could bridge two ingredients that did not typically go with each other if I paired them with an ingredient that went well with each separately. For instance, soy sauce and butter are opposed and don't mix well. But soy and lime go well together, and lime and butter are a fabulous combination. Here lime could bring these two opposing ingredients together. A lime-soy-butter emulsion is so simple and so delicious. Combine equal parts soy and lime in a pan, put it over medium-high heat, then swirl in an equal amount of butter. It makes a great all-purpose sauce for chicken or fish, and one to which any number of other elements can be added, depending on what the sauce is for. You might add some Dijon mustard if you're using it for pork, for instance.

We no longer had to follow all the rules from the French traditions. There was a single rule: *Flavor.* Flavor comes first.

I thought about food nonstop. I dreamed of food. I would come into the kitchen and tell one of my best chefs in those early days, Lois Freedman, "I dreamed a dish." And I had. A terrine of pasta and crabmeat. I would make a simple crabmeat farce, nothing more than crabmeat and cilantro, chopped to a paste so that it could be piped into cooked ziti. The stuffed ziti would be aligned in a terrine mold, then covered with a lobster broth flavored with lemongrass, lime juice, and harissa, and set with gelatin. Once it was thoroughly chilled and set, the crabmeat and macaroni terrine could be sliced and served with some lobster oil and a garnish of cilantro leaves. I loved this dish, one of my signatures back then. Though I'm not sure that Lois, in charge of filling hundreds of ziti every other day, adored it as much as I did!

Sushi was just taking off in New York City, which allowed me to create various versions of tuna tartare. I didn't invent the dish, but I loved the French original, steak tartare, which was often served with *frites*. Tuna would be lighter and more delicious, I figured, and I could pair it with so many new things. At first I served it, seasoned with olive oil and Tabasco, with *gaufrette* potatoes, the waffle-cut potato chips, and garnished it with chive oil. But in the new culinary landscape that was unfolding before my eyes, I soon realized that those potatoes could be any kind of chip—a beet chip, a lotus root chip, a fried basil leaf—and that the chive oil could be any oil, like bell pepper oil or curry oil.

Suddenly the possibilities were endless. After ten years of cooking Outhier's food, I had been liberated. Everyone in the kitchen felt the energy. We'd go on foraging trips to

Chinatown for lime leaves and galangal, and to the Union Square Greenmarket to find new key suppliers. The food was so new and so exciting that when Outhier came to visit, he didn't just taste the new dishes, he photographed them. We were killing it.

Soon a whole new philosophy emerged from these dishes, broken down according to the new building blocks I'd created.

It's important to remember, especially for young chefs starting out, that none of this would have been possible had I not been so solidly grounded in French technique. It had all begun in Monsieur Paul's pastry kitchen. You learn precision, and the rest follows. Picasso didn't wake up one morning and start painting in the cubist style. He first learned draftsmanship (after first learning how to properly clean his brushes and take care of the tools of his craft). Only after you've become a superlative draftsman do you have a chance to grow into a groundbreaking visual artist.

From the beginning, I worked clean and learned the fundamentals. This led to the great good fortune of being sent to the other side of the world to be introduced to a completely new, vibrant, and astonishing palate of flavors.

I then received an education in business, opening, after the Oriental hotel in Bangkok, seven restaurants in three years. I'd moved from a purely restaurant situation, in which someone else worries about the business, to the hotel environment, in which each restaurant within the hotel has its own food costs. So I had to know food costs, profit and loss statements, how the structure of restaurant deals works, not just how to butcher a skate wing, make a pan sauce, or the best way to cook white asparagus. This was a part of my education as well.

All these elements were set in place by 1986. They were my foundation. They framed my course. My muscles were strong and flexible from thirteen years of eighteen-hour days. I'd placed myself at the epicenter of the world's greatest restaurant city, at the most opportune moment in our culinary history. And then a critic had arrived to give me the biggest kick in the ass I'd ever had. To this day, I thank Gael Greene, and I tell her that she changed my cooking, my career.

The new flavors and philosophy I developed at Lafayette after the Gael Greene review were so effective, so powerful, that they lured the *New York Times* back for a second review just eighteen months after its initial three-star review, all but unheard of, to award us four stars. Lafayette became one of a select handful of restaurants in the city of New York to have earned this, the highest of rankings.

Does this *mean* anything to me? Are you kidding? I listen to critics. The night Miller's second review came out, I led my brigade through the kitchen banging pots and pans in celebration!

Learn the fundamentals so that you can then trust your instincts.

Shrimp Satay with a Wine-Oyster Reduction

I created this dish at Lafayette. Post–Gael Greene, I was always searching for the new thing to serve to customers who arrived *expecting* new and different dishes. This is one of our most beloved dishes and would move to Vong when we opened there. The original used an oyster sauce—a classic French reduction infused with Thai aromatics and finished with chopped oysters. We switched the sauce to a sweet-and-sour sauce for Vong, in keeping with that restaurant's commitment to full-on Southeast Asian cuisine. Here, I return to the original Lafayette sauce, the most basic of French sauces, a shallot-wine reduction mounted with cream. I throw a Thai chili into the shallots because I'm a bad boy and like the heat. I'll add my lime leaf and lemongrass for their aroma, cream it out, and then I'll finish the sauce with chopped oysters. This a great technique. The oysters give a great fresh sea taste, but also their protein helps to thicken the sauce and give it body.

I've never liked the propensity of shrimp to become overcooked and dry, especially in a restaurant kitchen, where so much is going on. To protect the shrimp, to keep them moist and succulent, I make a shrimp mousseline with coconut milk, fish sauce, and curry paste. I skewer the shrimp, making sure to tuck the tail under the fat end of the shrimp, forming a disk and protecting the very thin end of the tail. Then I season the shrimp with salt and cayenne, just a little—cayenne is the pepper I reach for first, not black pepper—and pipe the mousseline on top. I flip the shrimp and press them into the panko; then, with the shrimp still resting on the panko, I repeat the seasoning and piping on the top side as well. Then I flip the shrimp again and press the new mousseline side into the panko, though you should still be able to see the circumference of the shrimp between the layers of mousseline and panko.

When I think about where any new dish of mine comes from, I find that it's usually derived from something I made before. When I was a teenager working at Auberge de l'Ill, Monsieur Paul had a dish he called salmon soufflé. He made a salmon mousseline, much like the shrimp mousseline here, though he used cream, not coconut milk, and included egg whites. We coated a narrow pavé of salmon with this mixture and baked it. Because of the egg whites, the mousseline puffed up like a soufflé, protecting the salmon from overcooking and keeping everything very, very moist. Salmon loves gentle heat. A delicious dish.

But another preparation also came into play. In Thailand, I loved the fish cakes they made, *tod mun pla,* a puree of fish and curry paste and aromatics, fried.

These two ideas came together in my mind when I thought of ways to protect the shrimp from overcooking while making a more complex and interesting dish for my Lafayette menu. I would merge the pureed fish with fish sauce and curry to make a fish paste that could be fried (Thailand) with Monsieur Paul's classical salmon mousseline (France).

This dish works best with shrimp that are not so large (21–25 count), because it's easier to cook these shrimp without overbrowning the panko-covered mousseline.

It remains one of our favorite passed canapés, and made a fabulous course at Lafayette in the 1980s, especially with the oyster sauce.

First make the mousseline:

1 pound shrimp (21–25 count)
2 tablespoons fish sauce
1 tablespoon red curry paste
12 ounces coconut milk
Cayenne
Salt

Combine all but 12 of the shrimp in a food processor with the fish sauce, curry paste, and a splash of the coconut milk. Add a dusting of cayenne and a hit of salt. With the food processor running, pour the remaining coconut milk into the bowl in a thin stream until all of the ingredients are incorporated. I give it a taste here to make sure the seasoning is right, adjusting it as necessary with fish sauce. This is your mousseline. A classical mousseline would have shrimp, salt, egg white, and cream, so you can see the differences here—Thai aromatics and changing the fat to flavorful coconut milk. This is delicious as is. You could take this and make quenelles, dropping them off two spoons into simmering water or stock and cooking them as is, then serve them with the Thai shellfish base or the carrot juice sauce from the preceding recipe. But here, this mousseline will keep our sautéed shrimp juicy and delicious.

Next, make the sauce base:

> 1 tablespoon peanut oil
> 2 to 3 shallots
> Salt
> 1 Thai chili, bruised with the back of a knife to release the oils
> 2 Kaffir lime leaves, crushed between your fingers
> 2 stalks lemongrass, ends cut off, any dirty outer leaves removed, bruised with the back of a knife
> 2 cups dry white wine

Combine the oil and shallots in a saucier over medium heat. Give it a hit of salt. Add the chili, lime leaves, and lemongrass and sweat the mixture until the shallots are tender and the aromatics are fragrant. Add the wine, raise the heat to get it up to a simmer, then reduce the heat to keep it at a simmer and reduce it by half.

Now make the shrimp skewers:

> *Salt*
> *Cayenne*
> *Panko*
> *Grapeseed oil or clarified unsalted butter for*
> *   sautéing*

Preheat your oven to 350°F.

Fit the remaining 12 shrimp onto individual skewers so that they are in a tight curl with the tip of each tail beneath the fat end of the shrimp. Season them with salt and cayenne. Pipe about a tablespoon of the mousseline onto each, enough so that when you press them into the panko, the mousseline will spread out and cover the shrimp; the mousseline should be about a quarter-inch thick.

Press the mousseline side into a plateful of panko and leave them there. Season the top side of the shrimp with salt and cayenne, and pipe mousseline onto each. Turn them and press them into the panko.

Add a quarter inch of grapeseed oil or clarified butter to a large ovenproof sauté pan and place it over medium-high heat. Put the shrimp into the pan immediately, while the oil is still cold. If we were to put them into hot oil, the bread crumbs would become browned before the shrimp cooked. Once the oil comes up to heat and the shrimp are sizzling well, put the pan in the oven for a couple of minutes, just until they are nicely browned. Turn them, return them to the oven, and cook them until they're browned on the other side. You are going to turn your attention to the sauce here, but note that when you remove the shrimp, you should be able to see that they are solid white on the side, between the mousseline layers, and therefore cooked. When they are done, you will remove them to a paper-towel-lined plate to drain and rest.

While the shrimp are cooking in the oven, finish the sauce:

2 cups cream
5 or 6 oysters, shucked, roughly chopped
Salt
Cayenne
Lime juice

Add the cream to the reduced wine mixture and simmer till it's reduced by one-quarter. There's really not a lot to do here. It's a classical French sauce, but the Thai flavors make it very sexy. The shrimp should be done now and can be removed from the oven. Make sure both sides are nicely crisp and golden brown. When the cream has reduced, add the chopped oysters, stirring gently just to heat them through. Add a little more salt. Add a pinch of cayenne. Add several squeezes of lime juice, a little more than you think you should. Taste for seasoning.

Lime-leaf dust

I finish this dish with lime-leaf dust. Simply micro-wave a few Kaffir lime leaves at 30-second intervals until they're dry but still bright green. Pulverize them in a spice grinder. This is a great all-purpose garnish for French-Thai dishes.

Serve three shrimp skewers per plate or bowl. Divide the sauce among them. Dust with lime-leaf powder.

Et voilà: one of our favorite and most popular dishes.

SERVES 4

This dish remains as contemporary today as it was at Lafayette thirty years ago. At Vong it was a component of what we called the Black Platter, which also included lobster wrapped in a daikon sheet to make a roll, two spring rolls, and a tuna roll. Each had its own dipping sauce. For the lobster, I made a rosemary-ginger sauce. Oh my God, that was good! If you haven't tried this, do—rosemary and ginger, it's a magical combination.

BECOMING
A CHEF-
RESTAURATEUR

PART V

Lois Freedman decorating for New Year's Eve,
1988–89, at Lafayette. My brother Philippe
has just arrived from France to celebrate. In a
year he'd be working for me permanently.

14.

FIND A BALANCE
BETWEEN LOVE
AND WORK

IT'S IMPORTANT TO REMEMBER WHERE CUISINE WAS IN this country at the time, when my cooking style was on the verge of a dramatic change, as was the rest of the culinary world. As I mentioned earlier, American chefs were about to come into their own on the world stage, and that included French-born chefs such as Daniel Boulud and Gilbert Le Coze and myself. When I arrived in New York, the city had its Union Square Greenmarket. But it wasn't anything like it is today, a market teeming with farmers and a seemingly infinite variety of organic produce and hand-raised meats. Today the place is bursting with some of the best and most diverse plants and meats and dairy in the entire country. If you haven't been, it alone is worth a trip to New York City if you're a cook or love food.

But when I arrived in 1986, it was nothing like it is now. A smattering of stalls sold vegetables and fruit. There were maybe three different kinds of potatoes available, a few different varieties of apples and pears. Maybe some dried garlic. Some hearty lettuces. Today you can buy twenty-five different kinds of tomatoes, a wide variety of potatoes, five different colored beet varieties, several types of turnips, four colors of snow peas—yellow, green, dark green, and purple. And it's 80 percent organic. That's how much our country has changed in thirty years.

In 1986, I found most of my food in Chinatown. It wasn't organic, but it was pristine—beautiful carrots, glistening langoustines—and the vendors there had the rambutan and snake fruit I'd learned to cook with in Bangkok! I went to Chinatown every day.

It was also a time when the fear of fat was at its peak, and I knew New Yorkers wanted more chicken, which was considered more healthful. This was another reason to put a rotisserie in the kitchen: in order to be able to cook the number of orders I knew roast chicken would generate. Rotisseries were common in larger food-service operations, but not in restaurants. Our kitchen was in constant use. And soon I moved away from traditional *jus* and vegetables to spiking my *jus* with chili paste. Tony, my GM, loved it, and so did the customers.

To assure New Yorkers that they could get in, enjoy a four-star lunch and get out, we introduced what we called an express lunch menu, offering meals the kitchen could serve quickly—interesting salads and the rotisserie chicken, for instance.

In October of that year, a guy who was part of a catering company called Bink & Bink appeared in the restaurant with gorgeous raspberries. He'd been selling them at the market but still had many left over. I hadn't seen late-harvest raspberries here before and said yes, I'll take them. He explained that he was working with the growers at Jaxberry Farm, selling their produce, that he was just a middleman. I asked, "What else do they have?" He said, "What do you want?" And he handed me a seed catalog. "We can have anything you want by next year."

In this way, I began working with farmers to grow specifically for my menu. This was uncommon at the time. But there was a building movement of chefs working directly with farmers. Jean-Louis Palladin, from Gascony, was among the first. The Jones family began a new farm, the Chef's Garden, after their conventional farm was decimated by hail, recognizing that there was an untapped market in working with chefs.

The culinary world was changing, and we chefs in New York City were leading the way. It was an exciting time.

*

SO IT WAS, during this time of culinary foment, that I led my team at Lafayette. After we passed the three-year mark, in 1989, Outhier's contract with the Drake Hotel expired. With me so solidly at the helm of its restaurant Lafayette, cooking my own food, and having become better known than my mentor, the hotel didn't need to renew the contract or continue to pay Outhier. Part of the reason for this was that Outhier, thinking he could make all the money he needed by licensing deals, had closed L'Oasis. But once L'Oasis was shuttered, his name was no longer in demand. I had become better known in New York than he was. When the hotel directors informed me that they weren't renewing his contract, they asked if I would stay on as executive chef. I knew they needed me, so I said, "Sure. Pay me more money, upgrade my apartment, and we're good to go!" They agreed.

Once I became executive chef, and I was running my own show, I began to think about my status in the United States. I was married. I had two kids. I knew I needed a green card. I had a visa through the Drake Hotel, and I continued to ask my bosses to help me get my green card. They continued to tell me they were working on it. "It takes time, it takes time," they said. It eventually became clear that they were *not* working on it. They knew that once I had my green card, I'd be free to move elsewhere, so that's what was taking the time. They had me. I couldn't move on without a green card; that would be illegal. And I couldn't get a green card without their backing me.

With a wife and young children, I was in no position to change my circumstances, anyway. I continued to work eighteen-hour days, taking the elevator up to our apartment at midnight. I'd shower and turn on the TV, and be asleep in five minutes.

What was about to happen was partly my fault. I wasn't communicating with Muriel. When work was done, I didn't want to talk about my day; I didn't want to talk about the kids, as long as they were okay, about my wife, if she was okay. I need to recharge my batteries. I needed quiet and sleep. "Please don't ask me questions," I would say to Muriel. Though by nature I'm an introvert, my work requires that I talk to people all day, to my team, to the customers. The last thing I want to do when I finish work is to talk more. It's the nature of the work. So I was distant from my kids and from Muriel.

I was by now in my early thirties and very much a different person from the young chef I'd been when I lived and worked in Bangkok and we got married. She was different, too. I'd been cooking now for sixteen years. We'd both grown up, and we'd moved apart.

Balancing work and your personal life is a big task. You really do have to ask yourself, What's more important, my work or my private life? If you are a chef and have a spouse or partner who isn't understanding, it makes what is already hard work harder.

You could go the other way and engage in a relationship with a colleague, but should you? It's hard to say. I can't tell you, Don't do it. We have many couples who came together at our restaurants. When your boyfriend or girlfriend is in the business, you each understand the nature and demands of the work. But I've seen a lot of disasters, too. You're with each other all day long, twelve, fifteen, eighteen hours. It's demanding. Neither of you want to talk at the end of the day. If you work in different restaurants, your schedules may be different, and so you see each other even less. The restaurant life is hard, as you know.

In 1989, Muriel asked me for a separation and gave me an agreement to sign. I signed it. She wanted to live in France; I wanted to live in New York. I thought about moving to France to be with my kids, and I looked into work there. But it didn't make sense. I'd made my name in New York, not in France. Moreover, there was no way I could do my style of food in France. Cooking in France was still bound to the old traditions. America was producing some of the most exciting food in the world, and I was a part of that. New York was my home.

So I let her go and bought her a house in the south of France. This is where she still lives, and where she raised our children. I returned once a month to be with them. I missed them, but I was happy to be in New York.

Actually, more than happy. When my wife left me, suddenly I had more energy than ever before. I loved her, but she had made me worry. It had been stressful. When I was by myself, there were all kinds of new things I wanted to do.

Build my own restaurant, for instance.

With this new life, and new energy, I started going out in New York, I started enjoying life; I started dating Lois, one of my chefs. But there also came a feeling of oppression at Lafayette. Did I want to spend the rest of my life working for someone else?

No. That was easy. I did not.

And I'd begun to get smart about the restaurant business. When I had first started opening restaurants for Outhier, I hadn't cared about my food costs. The hotel picked everything up. The hotel executives weren't in the restaurant business to make money. The restaurants drew clients to their hotels, and they profited that way. And it was the same at Lafayette—at first. Every morning, someone, I don't know who, would drop off a sheet of paper detailing our expenses. I was always the first one in the kitchen, at seven-thirty, and there on the stainless steel table would be a sheet of paper showing how much we'd spent, how much we'd done in sales, how much food had been comped.

Once Outhier was out, and it was all me, I began to pay attention to this daily piece of paper. Our costs were all over the place. Generally speaking, a restaurant shouldn't spend more than about 30 percent of its total expenses on food. But sometimes our food cost would be 70 or 80 percent. My sous-chef, Pierre Schutz, and I began actively trying keep food costs down, and we found that we could. This was when I recognized how to make money in the restaurant business. During this phase, I turned Lafayette into a profitable business. In 1990, we had sales of $8 million (about $15 million in today's dollars), which was very good for a four-star French restaurant.

This was the key to my plan if I intended to make Lafayette my own.

I first asked the chairman of Swissôtel if he would let me take over the restaurant. I'd earned four stars. I'd made the restaurant famous. I made the company's executives a good offer. I said, "I'll give you ten percent of sales as rent, and I'll take on all the risk." They would thus be earning a lot of money at zero cost to them and would add nearly $1 million to their bottom line. But they said, "No, Lafayette is *our* baby." In fact, they were running a corporation owned by Nestlé and Swissair, which cared only about the bottom line, so none of it made sense. The people running the hotel didn't recognize that I was the one who had made the restaurant successful, not them. I couldn't convince them that it was in their best interest to let me take over the restaurant.

The savvy Gail Greene, having become a fan of my new cuisine, made a prediction in her column praising the new Lafayette: "How long will Swissôtel be able to keep this gifted wizard behind glass at the Drake?" she asked. "Probably not long."

I had to bite the bullet; otherwise I'd be a prisoner to them forever.

BLACK BEANS

FOIE GRAS

CHIVES point

BALSAMIC VINEGAR

LOTUS ROOT

This was a great Lafayette dish of sautéed foie gras on a
bed of black beans that had been stewed with foie gras fat,
almost like a cassoulet, so they were very rich. Garnished
with chives, lotus root chips, and balsamic vinegar.

15.

TAKE RISKS

ONE OF MY REGULAR CUSTOMERS AT LAFAYETTE WAS A businessman named Phil Suarez who'd taken an interest in the restaurant world. He invited me to help him consult with two men opening a steak house. I did, and he and I got along well. He eventually asked me if I wanted to open my own place. I told him I did. That day, he put $250,000 in an escrow account to show me how serious he was. When I was ready, that money would be, too.

In November 1990, I spotted a vacancy not far from the Drake, at Lexington and Sixty-fourth Street, on the Upper East Side. It was a beautiful little townhouse that had housed a series of restaurants since 1974. The latest restaurant there had filed for bankruptcy, and the space was available. I'd found my place. It was perfect.

The first thing I did was tell Phil. He said, "Great, let's sign the papers." So I gave the Drake notice and told Phil I was ready. We signed the lease for what would become JoJo in January 1991.

*

OF COURSE, I had no business signing anything. The Drake wouldn't renew my visa after I'd gone. I knew this, but I, well, *forgot* to mention it to Phil. What should I have done? I understood that Phil wouldn't sign those papers if he knew that my status was soon to be "illegal immigrant" and that I could get kicked out of the country. So I kept quiet. Risky, but it was the only way to achieve my goal of owning my own restaurant.

Once the lease was signed, we hired contractors and began to redo the space. I had moved into a small studio on the Upper East Side, between First and Second Avenues on East Seventy-sixth Street, a dreadful block. The apartment was tiny. But it was what I needed, just thirteen blocks from the restaurant. I slept on a futon on the floor for nearly a year. I was thirty-three years old. Ten years earlier, I had been living in Thailand with a chauffeur, a maid, and a cook. I'd become a four-star chef in Manhattan, making $100,000 a year in the 1980s—a considerable paycheck for a chef back then. Now I lived in a tiny fifth-floor walk-up, and I slept on a thin mattress on the floor. I made $500 a week. My life sucked. I ate pizza every night at Mezzaluna. I was desperately scared the whole time. I couldn't leave the country to see my children. I had no idea what the future held.

On the other hand, I understood that if my plans failed, I could always go back home, to Alsace, and cook there. And I knew that if I didn't take this gamble now, I never would.

While we were building the restaurant, I had time to take business courses, so that I would have a better idea about what I was doing once I began running my own business, something I'd never attempted before. A chef-restaurateur is half businessman, and you must learn these skills as well. I had to read up on the city and state requirements, what kinds of licenses I would need to operate a restaurant. The hotels I'd worked in had always taken care of business, and I'd hardly paid attention to these requirements. Now I personally needed to understand how business worked in America. For instance, in Europe, employers cut paychecks once a month; here it was once a week. Meeting payroll once a week is a lot of pressure. How, I wondered, did taxes work here? How much money did I need in the bank in order to open a business account? These were things I didn't know.

In April, less than four months after signing the lease, we were preparing to open the restaurant, having decided to name it JoJo, my nickname. We had no idea how it would do. Instead of going the luxurious route, I'd decided on something much more simple. An elegant bistro. Everyone was curious about what I would create after nearly two decades as a chef in Michelin three-star and *New York Times* four-star restaurants. Would I be bucking for four stars again? People presumed I would be.

But no—I'd decided to go in the *opposite* direction. I'd picked simple. Because that was what I believed people desired then. The economy had tanked in 1987, and a lot of the expensive business accounts had been axed. Many restaurants had pared down their menus. And this was what people wanted. I have a good sense of my customers—I listen to them, so that I can know what they want before *they* know they want it. This is not something that you can teach per se. A server must learn by watching, by paying attention. And by working with people who are good at it, experts, such as my brother Philippe. Over the years, you develop a sense of what your customers want, what pleases them, what irritates them. My customers wanted simplicity. And they always wanted new. They didn't want to pay the high prices I was used to charging at Lafayette, but they still wanted elegance and refinement in that simplicity. Also, the kitchen at JoJo was small, so I would be limited in what I could do—the menu had to be streamlined. I would be going from four-star dining, silver cloches, and starched tablecloths to *à la minute* cooking and paper tablecloths.

And for the time being, nobody knew what I was up to. Nobody even knew where I was.

Unlike the Lafayette kitchen, which was spacious, the kitchen at what would be JoJo had just six burners. I couldn't use them for long-simmered stocks—that wouldn't be practical. We would need them for cooking. So I resolved to rely on what had worked so well at Lafayette: juices, oils and vinaigrettes.

And I would keep the menu simple and small: six appetizers, six entrées, four desserts. Half were from Lafayette, half were brand-new. We'd stick with the molten chocolate cake, of course (see page 286 for the story and recipe).

To do very high-end food, you inevitably have a high food cost. I'd been spoiled by Lafayette, and now I had to turn my head around. I had to think practically. I had to maintain a tight control on costs. I wanted to keep prices down, as well. I'd started the shrimp with carrot juice at Lafayette but had moved on to doing it with lobster, in keeping with the upscale dining room. Here I'd go back to shrimp when I wanted such a dish. At Lafayette, I'd done a terrine of potato and foie gras. When the foie gras fat rendered during the cooking, the fat soaked into the potato— that was so good. But at JoJo, I'd replace the foie gras with goat cheese, serve it with a little arugula, arugula juice, and olive oil. Very simple, and this food would appeal to New Yorkers obsessing over grams of fat. No appetizer was more than twelve dollars, no entree more than twenty. There would be no caviar, no truffles. What I lacked in expensive ingredients, I would have to make up for in ingenuity. An important thing to remember.

I'd developed good relationships with the best suppliers during my years at Lafayette, so the quality of the food I could purchase was outstanding. I'd made friends with people at smaller boutique wineries I could rely on, and their bottlings were less expensive than those from the big châteaux. I didn't want to have *any* inventory. Whatever we bought, we sold. I didn't want any debt. So I was very smart with what I bought. I had no choice but to keep the kitchen staff to a minimum—just five of us, two on the hot line, one on garde-manger, one pastry chef, and me.

I would do a little of everything, garde-manger through desserts. I went from executive chef at Lafayette to what was basically a *commis*. I obsessed about everything. I was the one making sure the baguettes were warmed before they were served. Then I'd jump from garde-manger to the hot line to help those guys out. It was super-fast cooking. It had to be—on a busy Saturday night, we would do as many as three hundred covers.

But I didn't know whether it would be a success—everything was uncertain. I was nervous. I was in the country illegally. I was opening my first restaurant. The first time anything got out about what I was up to happened when someone walking down the street recognized me fussing with the outside windows. I told him, and word got around. Wine merchants knew I was putting together a wine list, and once I started buying wine, they figured we were getting ready to open. News travels fast in our little restaurant community.

That was all the publicity we needed. We were packed, absolutely packed, from day one. Day one. At five-fifteen nightly there was already a line forming at the door—I couldn't believe it. A few months after we opened, Bryan Miller reviewed us in the *Times*. I hoped for, at best, two stars for this casual bistro with paper tablecloths. And one would have been fine.

"In four visits to the two-month-old JoJo," Miller wrote, "I had the impression that something seminal was happening. JoJo is fueled by an ineluctable logic. Mr. Vongerichten serves food that looks and tastes great and is built on low-fat flavored oils rather than butter and cream. This is cooking for the 90's." And he gave JoJo *three* stars.

That review makes me so proud, but looking back, it's easy to see why the restaurant was successful. I'd scaled down—the menu offered items at a third of the price of Lafayette's, but with similar high-concept dishes. The bases were juices and broths, for a lighter style of cooking, which the country was craving. We'd created an elegant but casual setting that made people feel comfortable; New Yorkers had had enough of the overly formal French service. Affordable. Easy. Delicious. I had watched the customers at Lafayette, and I knew what they wanted now. (Lafayette closed not long after I left.)

I hope it's clear that the lesson here is all about flexibility. I went from the open Lafayette kitchen—with its silver cloches and gleaming copper pans and large open areas, it was the Taj Mahal of kitchens—to a 150-square-foot space mainly taken up by a central plating station and cooking areas, scarcely enough room for five cooks, let alone a team of servers running plates out to diners and back waiters returning them to the dishwashers.

But when I reflected further on it, I realized that this was not new to me. My mother had done all this with less. She'd served sixty people a day on four burners. I looked back to where I'd come from—a sixteen-year-old high school dropout—and thought, "This is amazing—look how lucky I've been." Six burners? How I could I complain? Six was a luxury! You start from there and keep making it bigger.

Then people began lining up every evening before we even opened the doors.

*

WITH THE RESTAURANT two months old and running smoothly, making money from its very first month, my mind could now turn to what had been bothering me but I hadn't been able to tell anyone. My ex-wife was putting pressure on me to visit the kids in France—but I couldn't. I wouldn't be let back into the country. Eventually, I became so stressed about this issue that I couldn't sleep. And I couldn't keep it from Phil any longer that I was an "illegal," an outlaw.

So at last I went to Phil. I told him, "Phil, I forgot to tell you one thing. It really bothers me. I can't sleep at night anymore."

He said, "What is it?"

I said, "I'm illegal."

He said, "*What?!*"

I said, "Yeah, my visa was because of the Drake Hotel. It's only good if I'm employed by them. I'm not in the country legally anymore."

"Are you crazy?" he screamed.

"We've been so busy," I said, "I didn't know what to do. But now that we're open, the place is packed. So? What do we do? I need to go see my kids for the weekend."

"You must be kidding!" he said. He was raking his hands through his hair, almost pulling it out. "Are you crazy?" he repeated. "Why didn't you *tell* me?"

"Because you would never have signed the lease!"

"Damn right I wouldn't have signed the lease!"

Once Phil calmed down, he said, "I'll find a way." And he did. He's brilliant. He gets things done. He called a lawyer he knew.

I went to see him. He looked at me and said, "What, are you crazy?"

But in the end, this lawyer was able to show immigration officials that I had created a successful, money-making, tax-paying business. I got a green card in a month.

Cod with Ketchup Sauce

(a.k.a. Roasted Cod, Vegetables Marinière with Sauce Aromates)

I'm going to admit it here for the first time. I wouldn't have put the word on my menu or offered the information, but the fact is, one of my best sauces at JoJo was made using ketchup. Yes, it's true. This, too, is part of being flexible. Again: I had only six burners; I could not afford to use up all that cooking real estate for stocks. Nor did we have the space to do *à la minute* fumets and *jus,* as I'd been doing since L'Oasis.

This is a classic JoJo dish, highlighted by a sauce using only bottled staples you can get at any grocery store. Remember, my kitchen was a 150-square-foot rectangle into which were shoehorned all countertops, cook surfaces, the pass, and the three main stations—garde-manger, hot line, and pastry—as well as the dishwasher's station. Three hundred covers a night out of that little closet of a space. I had to be crafty with the sauces, which had originally been stock-based when I'd had plenty of space in Lafayette's kitchen, a palace in comparison to JoJo's space. So I created this: ketchup, red wine vinegar spiked with Tabasco (I love Tabasco, one of America's oldest prepared sauces), and soy sauce, all brought together with plenty of butter.

Again, I looked to one of my previous preparations, then simply swapped ingredients. Remember the soy-butter-lime sauce I mentioned? A simple emulsion of those three ingredients is great on all fish and chicken. This would be the same thing. The only things I did differently were to change the acid from lime to red wine vinegar, seasoned with Tabasco, and add fish sauce. But the idea is the same: butter emulsifying the soy and vinegar. To give it color, body, and more flavor, ketchup! It's amazing. I love ketchup. This base could be made in the morning and be ready to reheat and serve whenever I needed it. I called it my *sauce américaine*! Traditional *sauce américaine*, a French classic, is a tomato-based sauce usually used for lobster or other shellfish. You would never find soy sauce in such a preparation, so this is my nouveau version using only bottled American sauces. On the menu at JoJo, so that people wouldn't confuse this with the traditional French sauce, I simply called it *sauce aromates*.

It's dead simple. You can use it just as is. At the restaurant, I wanted a ratatouille-style garnish, so while the sauce is simple, the garnish is a nightmare. (More than a dozen ingredients!) Feel free to use whatever is on hand and tailor your garnish to the ingredients you have and the time you have—ideally, there will be a sweet vegetable, a salty component, and an aromatic component. Because this was a three-star dish, I went all out: brunoise of blanched and shocked fennel, zucchini, celery, and red and orange peppers, along with a brunoise of tomato, oil-cured black olives, and bright green Castelvetrano olives, plus capers, thyme leaves, a minced Thai chili, Thai basil chiffonade, and, importantly, saffron.

Prepare everything ahead of time: about ¼ cup of each of the vegetables, a tablespoon each of the salty ingredients, ¼ teaspoon of the herbs, and the saffron, which is great for color and flavor in Provençal dishes.

Also three-star cooking: an optional decorative flourish of herb oil.

Parsley
Chives
Basil
Olive oil
Salt

Blanch and shock the herbs, then puree them with the olive oil and a hit of salt and strain the mixture. (True to the JoJo philosophy of letting nothing go to waste, we add the strained herbs from the puree to pureed potatoes for an herb-potato side dish.) The oil makes for a great presentation and seasoning if you want to go to the effort. Make this ahead of time as well.

To finish the garnish:

1 clove garlic, minced
1 small onion, cut into small dice
½ cup olive oil
Salt

Sweat the garlic and onion in the olive oil, hitting them with some salt. They should fry in the oil. When the garlic and onion are simmering and hot and very soft, remove the pan from the heat. Add whatever vegetables you wish for garnish. Here's what we use (as mentioned above, the fennel, zucchini, celery, and bell peppers should have been blanched and shocked so that they're tender):

½ fennel bulb, cut into brunoise
½ zucchini, cut into brunoise
2 celery stalks, cut into brunoise
1 red pepper, cut into brunoise
1 orange pepper, cut into brunoise
1 small tomato, peeled, seeded, and cut into brunoise
10 oil-cured black olives, pitted, cut into brunoise
10 Castelvetrano olives, pitted, cut into brunoise
1 tablespoon capers
Thyme leaves from one twig of thyme
1 Thai chili, minced
2 Thai basil leaves, cut into chiffonade
Pinch of saffron

Toss everything together to warm it all through. Set the mixture aside and keep it warm.

Make the sauce:

> 4 ounces ketchup
> 3 ounces soy sauce
> 3 ounces red wine vinegar
> 1 teaspoon Tabasco
> 10 ounces unsalted butter

Combine everything except the butter in a saucier over medium-high heat. When the ingredients are combined and just beginning to simmer, add the butter in chunks, whisking continuously until the butter is melted and emulsified into the sauce.

And that's all, two minutes on the stove. Look at it. It's got the depth of color of a long-simmered stock-based sauce. Taste it. A fabulous all-purpose concoction for fish, chicken, shellfish, even rice. Just before serving the sauce, because it can be very rich and unctuous, I give it a buzz with the hand blender to lighten it.

To finish the dish:

> Four 4-ounce fish filets (cod, hake, or other
>   white flaky fish)
> Salt
> Grapeseed or olive oil

Season the fish with salt and sauté it in the oil over medium-high heat just until it's warm in the center, a couple minutes per side. (In the restaurant we'd flip it and finish it in the oven.) Remove it to a plate lined with paper towels while you spoon warm sauce onto the plates, and rim the sauce with the herb oil, if using. Set a piece of fish in the center of each plate. Spoon a ½-inch-thick layer of the ratatouille vegetable garnish over the top of the fish. Top with a couple of fresh basil leaves or thyme sprigs, if you wish.

SERVES 4

And there it is. A dish created to accommodate JoJo's 150-square-foot kitchen in 1991, three hundred covers daily, and still on our classics menu once a week today.

16.

LET THE SPACE
DETERMINE THE MENU

I HAD TAKEN THE HUGE RISK OF OPENING JOJO (LIVING on $500 a week in a fifth-floor walk-up studio with a futon mattress on the floor) out of a desperation to leave Lafayette and to be independent. With ingenuity, frugality, and, most importantly, flexibility, we'd turned the restaurant into an instant success. Phil was a great partner, and I'd convinced my younger brother Philippe to leave his job in France as a carpenter to help me rebuild the space. (Who could have known he would become the extraordinary teacher and front-of-the-house leader at my flagship just six years later?) As we were creating JoJo, I was so excited, so happy. I felt that this was going to be my home, this would be my life. It would be like André Soltner and Lutèce. He'd opened his iconic French restaurant fourteen blocks south of JoJo in 1961, and he was still going strong when I opened thirty years later. It would be my Auberge. I would have the same sort of arrangement Monsieur Paul had. JoJo, nine blocks from Lafayette, would be my home.

After six months, JoJo was looking about as interesting as a double-decker bus. It was a tiny restaurant, with two rooms on two levels. The kitchen was confining. Six burners, one oven, one salamander, one little fryer. I looked at the kitchen, at the menu—there was really not enough room to do more than six, maybe eight, entrées.

"Man," I began to think at the end of the night. "Am I really going to spend my *life* here? *I have so many ideas, so many things I want to do.*"

But you don't stop working, ever—you keep on cutting, keep heating the baguettes for service, keep on tending to the customers, watch who's lining up at the door. I was the chef and a *commis* in one. Still, day after day, doing the same food, in the same small place, serving it in the same small rooms, I began to think, "My God, I could *die* in this place." It made my head spin. For ten years I'd worked at a high pitch, opening ten restaurants, earning four stars in Boston, then four stars in New York, and now I had created what the *Times* had called a "seminal" restaurant. I couldn't just stop striving. But, I also thought, "I don't think I can stay in one place. I really will die."

Then one day . . . a young architect and designer named David Rockwell called me. I'd known him at Lafayette, where he'd brought clients. He mainly did interior design for wealthy New Yorkers, but he'd also done one high-profile restaurant, Arizona 206; he'd liked the experience and wanted to do another. He followed me from Lafayette to JoJo. And one day he called me and said, "Hey, JG, you interested in a new space?"

I said, "Yes, David! Oh my God, *yes*! Where, what, how? What can we do?!"

"There's this Italian space called Toscana, in the Lipstick Building, Fifty-third and Third. They're going out of business. I'm talking to the parent company that owns the building, Hines. They built it five years ago. Do you want to take it over?"

I immediately went to see the space, on the ground floor of an oval office tower (hence the building's nickname). I studied the curved walls of the restaurant, the high ceiling. It looked not like an Italian restaurant but, rather, like a temple, a *Thai* temple. Before arriving, I hadn't had any preconception of the kind of restaurant I might want to open there. But I knew as soon as I was standing in the space what it should be. I called David and asked, "Can you design something like an Asian temple?" It looked Asian to me, not Italian—its spirit was Asian. All the wood, the gold-leaf ceiling. In my head, I immediately had this Thai-French fantasy. So David designed and built me a temple that reminded me of my years in Bangkok, and he would go on to become one of the most sought-after restaurant designers in the city.

But it was my Bangkok. I had returned to the place that had shaped me.

And this was how Vong was created. I began to design the food according to what the space told me. I didn't realize it at the time, but this was how I would always open my restaurants in terms of the food. I would never write the menu until the restaurant was designed. That's how important place is to the food people consume in that space. Remember this.

I'm a big believer in feng shui. It's an important fact of successful restaurants. And I always pay attention to the details, everything from the decor to how light falls on the tables. I will fly across the country to look at chairs a designer wants to use, to touch them, sit in them. (If I hadn't become a chef, I might have returned to school to become an architect. I love the precision combined with the creativity.) This is part of feng shui. Feng shui, so prominent in Asia, is part commonsense practicality and part mystical belief, a measure of the overall harmony and energy of a place.

I do believe in the mystical part. I believe there's an energy in the universe we can't fully know. I have a friend, Jerome Brasset, who practices the ancient occult practice of geomancy, a form of spirit reading. Jerome makes a daily calendar for me, and I stick to it; if it says do not make important business decisions during this week, I don't; if it tells me don't fly on this day, I'll rearrange my schedule to avoid flying. I know, having followed Jerome's advice, that I sleep like a baby when my bed is facing northeast; I sometimes rearrange the bed in my hotel room to face this direction. As I told Rick Marin of the *New York Times,* "I don't make a move without him." And I believe in that element of feng shui that may seem beyond the rational. But there is also the practical element of feng shui in restaurants: Does this restaurant sit on a corner where turning cars will shine headlights into the faces of diners? Does the wind regularly blow against the opening of the entrance door?

And since I was a boy, putting lamps on the basement floor to prepare for a party, I have loved the design component of entertaining. At Vong, I created a display of all the Asian spices and ingredients we'd be using, so people could see them—I knew they wouldn't be familiar with them, with galangal, fresh turmeric. I foresaw how powerful the curved wall might be, and so I covered it with Asian newspaper clippings, maps of Asia, and fabric swatches, to evoke Southeast Asia of the 1970s, which remained so powerful in America's consciousness because of the Vietnam War, and had been refreshed in the mind of New Yorkers with the success of the Broadway musical *Miss Saigon*.

Again, context is important here. This was more than twenty-five years ago. New York had Chinese restaurants, the authentic ones primarily in Chinatown. Shun Lee Palace, in midtown, was pretty good. And there were plenty of mom-and-pop restaurants serving Thai food along Eighth Avenue. There were a few Japanese restaurants, but there was no Nobu. There was almost nothing, except perhaps the French-Vietnamese Indochine downtown, that served anything close to what I was about to serve and in the style that I was accustomed to, having come of age in Michelin three-star restaurants. Vong would be an entirely new creation, unique among Manhattan restaurants.

I could return in my heart and in my mind to Bangkok, use it to fully infuse my French training. One of the first things I put on the menu was the foie gras with mango, which remains a fantastic pairing. I paired lobster with peppery turnip and served it with a honey-ginger vinaigrette. I reimagined the Thai lobster Outhier and I had worked on. I seasoned duck stock with lime for an egg noodle soup with duck and topped it with crispy noodles. I re-created the coconut milk and chicken soup I'd tasted my first hour in Bangkok, seasoned with lemongrass and hot chilies. We made fabulous crab spring rolls in sheets of rice paper, wrapped in lettuce and served with another vinaigrette, this one using tart tamarind. I put peanut sauce on charred squid and greens. No one had seen these combinations before.

I now had my temple, the perfect place to fulfill my vision of a completely Asian-French fusion menu. It would be original, and the flavors would focus everything I'd learned in Southeast Asia, the lemongrass and chilies and herbs, focus it like sun through a magnifying glass. A reservation at Vong, according to the *Times*' three-star review in February 1993, was "the hottest ticket in town."

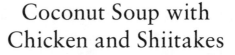

Coconut Soup with Chicken and Shiitakes

Vong arrived with a bang in 1992, and this is one of the first dishes I created for it; it would also be on the Vong London menu. Make it and your kitchen will smell like Thailand. Ever since I'd arrived in New York and had begun to infuse vegetable juices with lime leaves and lemongrass, I'd known that I wanted to create a restaurant that served French–Southeast Asian cuisine. This is the epitome of the style. I still serve this soup at Mercer Kitchen.

This dish begins by sweating a lot of aromatics in chicken stock. Sometimes I tie them all up in cheesecloth, so that they can be removed once they've infused the stock. But sometimes I just freestyle it and leave them all in. What you choose to do can depend on your mood. I like leaving whole stalks of lemongrass in a soup. You don't eat them, but they're delicious to chew on. I also add a chicken carcass to the aromatics, sweating that as well to fortify the stock. If you're using a carcass, it should cook in the stock for an hour or so. Again, this depends on your mood, how much time you have, who you are cooking for. Both methods work!

I think the most important aromatic here is the fresh galangal, a rhizome, like ginger, and similar to ginger in appearance but quite different in flavor. Smell a freshly cut piece and you will see that it has an almost eucalyptus-like quality. If you can't find galangal, there's no reason you can't make this soup with ginger. It will still be delicious, just not quite the same.

I can't resist adding butter to the stock while it infuses with the aromatics. Butter makes everything better.

I finish it with coconut milk and cook the chicken and mushrooms *à la minute*.

Combine the following in a medium saucepan over medium heat:

1 large onion, sliced
1-inch piece galangal peeled and thinly sliced
2 tablespoons red curry paste
2 tablespoons unsalted butter
1 raw chicken carcass (optional)
Salt

Stir and cook everything together, seasoning with salt as you do. Cover the pan to speed up the sweating. Your kitchen should begin to smell like a Thai kitchen from the galangal and curry!

6 cups chicken stock

When the onions have sweated well and are tender but not browned, add the stock.

Wrap the following in cheesecloth to create a sachet, if you wish. If you don't want to, don't. Instead, you can strain the soup before you add the garnish (we use a sachet at Mercer Kitchen) or, again, serve it freestyle, as they do in Thailand.

2 Kaffir lime leaves, bruised by hand
1 bunch cilantro stems
2 cloves garlic
2 to 3 Thai chilies, smashed or bruised
1 stalk lemongrass, smacked many times with back of a chef's knife to cut and crush it and release its flavors
1 raw chicken carcass or 5 or 6 chicken wings (optional; if using, don't include this in the sachet)

Add everything to the stock and continue to simmer for 20 to 30 minutes (or up to an hour at a very low temperature to get the most out of the chicken bones, if you're using them). Remove and discard the sachet and chicken bones or strain the mixture into a new pot. Add the following to your soup:

> *2 cups coconut milk*
> *8 shiitake mushrooms, quartered or cut into*
>   *large chunks*
> *1 pound chicken breast, large dice*
> *Lime juice to taste—start with 1 tablespoon*
>   *and taste from there*
> *Fish sauce to taste—start with 1 tablespoon*
>   *and taste from there*

As the mushrooms and chicken cook, taste the soup. It should be pungent with lime juice. You should be able to taste a hint of the fish sauce. Cook it until the chicken is just heated through. Divide into bowls and garnish with:

> *Scallions, thinly sliced*
> *Cilantro leaves*
> *1 Kaffir lime leaf each*

Serve the soup with jasmine rice on the side. To eat it as they do in Bangkok, take a spoonful of rice and dip it into the soup. I could eat this soup every day.

SERVES 4

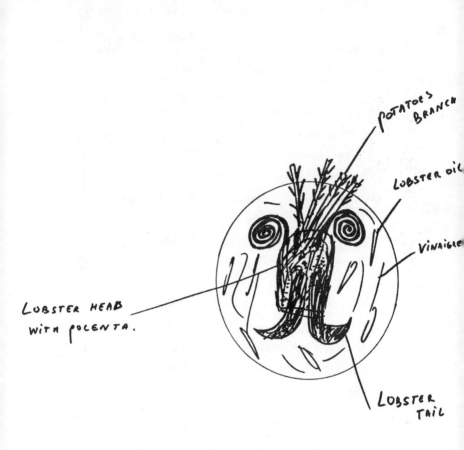

POTATOES BRANCH

LOBSTER OIL

VINAIGRE

LOBSTER HEAD
WITH POLENTA.

LOBSTER
TAIL

Another Lafayette dish, lobster with polenta and
rosemary potatoes (rosemary leaves stuck into the potato
batons, lobster oil, and a vinaigrette). We cooked the
head so that the antennae remained perfectly curled.

17.

LEARN THE UNSPOKEN RULES OF YOUR CITY

OPENING VONG, MY SECOND RESTAURANT, WAS PROBA-bly the hardest thing I've ever done, *because* it was my second restaurant. I was lucky that Vong and JoJo were in the same part of the city, since I was forever running back and forth between the two. I thought, "Who will make sure the baguettes are served warm?"

I suppose that every chef who has opened multiple restaurants will tell you that the second one was the hardest point in the expansion. That's when you have to learn to give up control, learn to delegate, ensure that you've created a strong team to handle both the front of the house and the back of the house. I kept my team from Lafayette: Ron Gallo, Lois Freedman, and Pierre Schutz all stayed with me for the long haul. And Danny Del Vecchio—he'd been hounding me for a job since Lafayette, and I finally had a spot for him. All of them remain part of my team—I don't know what I'd do without them. And, of course, my brother Philippe also proved to be invaluable. He came to help me build JoJo but would become a true partner and our primary front-of-the-house leader.

I'd gotten a taste of running two food businesses because before we could open Vong, we had to take over the café in the Lipstick Building. This was part of the condition of acquiring the Toscana space. Opening this simple-concept spot helped me make the jump to running two restaurants. So we opened the café first. This was an immediate success, but how could it not have been? We were the only place in the building to get food, and there weren't a lot of good options in the neighborhood at the time.

I was beginning to solidify my name in New York City, and Vong was packed from the beginning, even before the *New York Times* gave it a three-star review. Of course, in the restaurant business generally, and in New York especially, there's always something. We ran into a little hiccup unique to the city—a situation I'd never encountered before but from which I would learn!

Because the Lipstick Café and, especially, Vong were both so successful, we were generating far more trash than the building was used to.

In New York, restaurants pay a lot of money for daily garbage pickup. At the Lipstick Building, we were paying $3,500 a month for the service just with the café. But after Vong opened and began doing three hundred covers a day, I got a letter from the company's managers telling me they were now going to charge me $5,000! I told them that I refused to pay $5,000 for garbage pickup. And so they stopped collecting. For three days, I had no garbage pickup. The building had to contact me to tell me the loading dock was overflowing with smelly garbage and I needed to do something about it.

So I called the company that handled JoJo, told them

the story, and they said, "Are you sure you want us to do this? You want us to collect your garbage?" They knew it was a bad idea, but I didn't. I said, "Yes, I'm sure." And they said, "Well, all right, if that's what you want." And they started the next day. Problem solved.

A couple days later, I was in Vong's dining room, just before we were about to open for business, when eight enormous goombahs walked in. They were dressed in gar-bagemen's clothes, filthy, stinking, and one guy had a big meat hook over his shoulder. I went to hide in the kitchen, pretending to be busy. The manager came back and told me they had no intention of leaving until I spoke with them.

I had no choice but to go talk to them. They wanted more money. They told me right there, "You don't want to pay us our money? You want to use another company? Okay. We'll send you back to France. In a coffin."

That, my friends, is the New York City way.

So. I paid them. Sure, I was scared. This wasn't a set of tires. They weren't kidding!

My mistake, which I understand now, was in not nego-tiating. That's what's expected. They didn't think I'd pay $5,000. I should have negotiated. But I paid what they asked. And that's how the goombahs roll.

In this way, I learned the rules of restaurant life in New York City. Every place you go will have its own rules and customs and culture; you must learn and respect different cultures rather than try to impose your will on them.

Despite this setback, we hit our groove. I now had two major successes, and I had surmounted one of the chef's greatest hurdles: opening the second restaurant. Even bet-ter, it was a second restaurant doing my favorite food, food

I felt so comfortable with. Coconut soup—that was my life. Plus the Thai lobster and the shrimp sauté. I'd been practicing these dishes, after all, at Lafayette, though in a more tempered way. Now I could go at it full steam, put into action a menu I'd been building in my mind for four years. (Don't be surprised if you see its return one day.)

18.

MAKE YOUR OWN OPPORTUNITIES

SINCE SETTING OUT ON MY OWN WITH JOJO AND VONG, I've opened dozens of restaurants outside New York and outside the country. These are exclusively licensing deals, something I'll describe in more detail later because they've been so important to me, now accounting for 75 percent of my company's business. Given the way gastronomy has developed throughout the world (remember, Outhier began to expand in 1980), my company's growth was assured as long as I remained successful in Manhattan. But for me, expansion began by pure chance, because I'd fallen in love. It's true. But it's also a lesson in saying yes to opportunities that come your way and being flexible.

She was half American, half British. She'd worked the front of the house at Vong, although then she'd returned to London to attend law school. One weekend I flew over to visit her. JoJo was still going strong, and the Lipstick Café and Vong had been open for two years and were likewise thriving. My staff was solid. I was able to leave the restaurants to take time off to visit her. I'd gotten us a room at the Four Seasons, and our first morning there, I ordered breakfast from room service. We waited. And waited. Eventually my girlfriend had to leave for class, hungry. The food arrived an hour and fifteen minutes after we'd ordered it, and I ate alone.

Our room was on the tenth floor, and on my way to the lobby later that morning, the elevator stopped at the fifth floor. An employee of the hotel got on. He asked me how I was enjoying my stay. I told him I was enjoying it, but that breakfast had taken more than an hour to get to my room. The man apologized, then explained that he was the general manager of the hotel. We exchanged cards. It turned out that he knew of JoJo, had *been* to Vong in New York and had loved it. In fact, he had something he'd like to discuss with me—could he buy me a drink that evening? I said sure.

That night at the bar, he explained his idea. The restaurant at the hotel was moribund. He needed to do something to give it some juice. He asked me if I would do a Vong promotion there. It was 1994, and the concept of pop-up restaurants didn't have a name yet, but that's essentially what he was suggesting, only *he* would be paying *me*. He offered me twenty grand, said he'd fly my team over first-class. I'd be able to see my girlfriend, promote my restaurant, and earn a little cash. So I agreed, enthusiastically.

Three months later, I brought three of my guys and we prepped as we did for Vong in New York, where we did 150 covers for lunch, 250 for dinner. The hotel had taken out full-page ads in the local newspapers. We were ready.

I think about twenty people came for lunch, twenty-five for dinner. I asked the general manager, "What's going on?" He had no idea. And I thought to myself, "Shit, look at all this food. We have enough to feed eight hundred people. I've got to get people into the restaurant or we're going to lose money and food."

The next morning I arrived at the restaurant early. I sat at the bar having a coffee, trying to figure out how to promote what we were doing. I kept hearing a phone ringing. And ringing. I realized it was at the front desk and there was no one answering it. Finally, *I* got up to answer the phone, and it was someone calling to make a reservation. People wanted to come to our pop-up, but no one had been answering their calls!

I stood at the front desk for the next two hours, taking reservations. In that short span, I took eighty lunch reservations and 120 reservations for dinner.

And the manager freaked out.

"What are you doing, taking so many reservations?" he shouted. "We can't serve that many people!" They had never done these kinds of numbers before. I told him, "Look, it's not worth my time to do thirty covers. I want people in London to see what I do, I want them to have my Thai lobster and foie with mango." London was a culinary backwater at the time. The city needed to see what was happening in New York.

"Relax," I told him. "*We . . . do* know how to cook for and serve this many people. This is what we do."

And we did. We crushed it. We did three hundred covers a day for the rest of the week. Our first pop-up was a success. And the staff at the Four Seasons loved it, too. They'd never made so much in tips.

We were so busy in New York when we got back, I didn't think any more about the pop-up. But a few months later, the GM I'd met in the elevator called me to say that he'd left the Four Seasons and was now managing director of the Savoy Group, which managed some of London's best hotels, including Claridge's, the Connaught, and the Berkeley. The Berkeley, he told me, happened to have a dead space in it. He asked me if I wanted to open a Vong there.

It was just like that call from David Rockwell a few years earlier. I thought, *"Hallelujah!" Immediately* I know this is a great idea.

But more important than recognizing that it was a great idea was knowing *how* to do it. I knew how to open a restaurant. That was all I had done for five years, open restaurants in hotels for Outhier in foreign countries. I could do this with my eyes closed. Also, and more importantly, I knew how to structure a licensing deal. I'd learned this from working so closely with Outhier and paying attention as I moved from Bangkok to Singapore, then to Japan, to Geneva, to Lisbon, to London, to Boston, to New York, and now I'd come back to London. I said, "You give me six percent of the top, ten percent of the bottom"—meaning gross sales and net sales, respectively— "as well as a signing fee, let us design it, and I'll do it." Six months later, at the end of 1995, we opened Vong London.

It wouldn't have happened had I not gone to London to visit a woman. It might not have happened if breakfast had been on time or I'd taken a different elevator. It was pure chance. But there's this, too: I said yes. I could have argued that it was too much work, that we were slammed in New York, that I couldn't afford to have my guys away for a week. Because expansion is hard, and it does take work. But this is what I do. I say yes. And, approaching age forty, I had the experience and flexibility I needed to accomplish it.

So: pay attention to chance, be flexible, and say yes to opportunities when they come to you.

Les Hors-d'Oeuvre

Terrine de Queue de Boeuf aux Jeunes Poireaux à l'Huile de Raifort
Oxtail Terrine Wrapped in Baby Leek and Horseradish Oil

Salade de Germes de Soja aux Crevettes de Louisiane
Warm Louisiana Shrimp and Soya Sprouts Salad

Marinade de Haricots Secs et Frais au Filet de Pigeon Rosé
Marinated Mixed Beans with Roasted Squab Breast

Salade de Foies et Rognons de Lapereau aux Navets Crus et Cacahuètes
Salad of Raw Turnips and Peanuts with Rabbit Kidney and Liver

Pommes de Terre Nouvelles en Salade et Grillons de Ris de Veau au Foie Gras
Crisp Sweetbread on New Potato Salad with Foie Gras

Saumon Frais aux Palourdes et la Vinaigrette d'Huîtres
Clams and Cucumber Wrapped with Fresh Salmon, Oyster Vinaigrette

Tartare de Thon aux Légumes de Printemps Frits
Tuna Tartar with Crisp Spring Vegetables

Saint-Jacques aux Vermicelles d'Artichaud, Fèves et Sarriette
Maine Scallops with Artichoke Vermicelli and Fava Beans

Flan d'Oursins aux Crêpes de Petits Pois et Caviar
Sea Urchin Flan with Green Pea Pancakes and Caviar

Soupe de Gyromitres Fraîches aux Herbes de Printemps
Gyromitre-Morel Soup Flavored with Fresh Herbs and Asparagus

Bigorneaux et Moules en Coupe de Riz et Nage de Légumes
Vegetable Broth with Periwinkles and Mussels in Rice Paper

Les Entrées

Saumon et Palourdes Sautés à la Laitue, Rillons de Canard
Rare Salmon with Stewed Clams and Lettuce

Sandre Pochée à Four Doux, Rémoulade de Céleri et Huile de Curry
Poached Yellow Pike with Celery Root and Curry Oil

Homard Braisé au Jus de Carottes Épicé et Coriandre (88.00)
Maine Lobster Braised in Spiced Carrot Juice and Coriander

Black Bass à la Purée au Vin Rouge et Betteraves Croquantes
Black Bass Fillet in Wine Potato Purée and Beet Root Chips

Flétan aux Fèves à l'Huile de Truffe et Poivrons Jaunes
Halibut with Fava Beans, Truffle and Yellow Pepper

Cabri Rôti à la Broche, aux Panisses et Aubergines Marinées
Spit Roasted Baby Goat with Chick Pea Pancake and Marinated Eggplant

Selle de Veau aux Concombres, Cornichons et Poivre Szechuan
Saddle of Veal with Cucumbers, Gherkins and Szechuan Pepper

Pintade Marinée au Citron et Herbes Printanières
Marinated Guinea Hen with Lemon and Spring Herbs

Pastilla de Canard Éclatée au Blé Concassé
Bursting Pastilla of Duckling and Cracked Wheat

Râble de Lapin Rôti au Coriandre, Riz Basmati aux Fruits et Curry
Roasted Filled of Young Rabbit with Coriander, Basmati Rice with Fruit and Curry

Roulade de Chèvre et Pommes Nouvelles à l'Huile de Ciboulette (27.50)
Goat Cheese and Potato Roulade with Chive Oil

Les Desserts   Les Sorbets et Glaces
A Variety of Desserts   Homemade Sherbet and Ice Cream

Café — Espresso — Cappuccino
Le Dîner $65.00

[handwritten notes] SAUTÉ the SCHRIMP ADD SCHALLOT DEGLAZE SOYA SAUCE REMOVE IN A BOLL ADD SOYA SPROUT HAZEL NUT OIL SEASON SALT + PEPPER

LEMON JUICE YOGOURT + CREAM SEASO. V

MARINADED MUSHROOM

SOYA BEANS

SCHRIMP + SOYA SPROUT

This is an early menu from Lafayette, before the Gael Greene review, but notice that I'm already thinking ahead, using it to scratch out an idea for a new dish. Shrimp is sautéed with some shallot, deglazed with soy. Add bean sprouts, peanuts, and chive buds. Serve with mushroom tossed with a yogurt-cream seasoned with lemon, salt, and pepper. Garnish with blanched beans, mint, and cilantro. The plating diagram is to the right. It was a dish that would last through to Vong.

19.

DO WHAT YOU'RE
BEST AT

EVERYTHING WAS GOING BEAUTIFULLY, THE RESTAU-
rants were packed and making money, my staff was solid,
and my partner, Phil, was happy. And yet. Something was
missing. I hadn't touched truffles in years. Or caviar. I
missed that. I had started my career in a Michelin three-
star and spent the first seventeen years of my working life
working in the highest echelons of fine dining. I knew I
needed to return to that.

Also, things were heating up in New York City. Le
Bernardin was going strong; ten years earlier, when I'd
first arrived in America, it had been the only restaurant to
earn four stars from the *New York Times* straight out of
the gate. With Lafayette closed, David Waltuck at Chan-
terelle, Daniel Boulud at Daniel, and Gray Kunz at Lespi-
nasse were the only other four-star chefs in the city. The
Zen-like Thomas Keller was putting out some uncommonly original food at the French Laundry, in Yount-
ville, California. The whole culinary scene, from coast
to coast, was making huge leaps forward. Even in the

heartland of the country, Cleveland, Detroit, Milwaukee, Denver, cities not known for their food, young chefs were opening dynamic new restaurants supported by patrons and a culture that was beginning to truly embrace innovative cuisine.

I'm competitive by nature. So I wanted to get back in the game. I wanted to see what I could do, now, in the high-end arena I'd left more than five years earlier. And I wanted to do it in Manhattan, the toughest restaurant city in the world.

The Lipstick Building, where I had the Lipstick Café and Vong, had been designed by Philip Johnson, one of the premier architects of the twentieth century. He'd moved his offices there when the building was completed, in the mid-1980s. The man was eighty years old at the time. A decade later, I would open my café and restaurant. Johnson, still going strong, ate at the café every day. When he wanted to get away from all the people in his office, he would come to the café to think, and because of that, I got to know him. Wonderful man.

One day he called me over and showed me his designs for a new hotel and condominium building going up on Columbus Circle. He pointed to the area closest to the circle and said, "See this corner? This is for you."

I said, "What do you mean?"

He said, "The building needs a restaurant. It should be yours." He gave me his card.

I gave the card to my partner. Phil called Philip Johnson's office, and soon we were touring the space. The building was owned by General Electric. Donald Trump would soon be asked to put his name on it and take over its management. But our moving in was not a given. Other restaurateurs and chefs made a play for the space as well. Drew Nieporent, the force behind Montrachet, and his chef, my friend David Bouley, wanted it. Drai's, a popular restaurant and nightclub then based in Los Angeles, was Trump's choice.

But we made our case. I told the GE board that I intended to create a gem, New York City's next four-star restaurant. I did it at the Drake, I said, and I can do it here. Plus, I knew the hotel food business from having worked in hotels for the first half of my career. I hadn't done room service, but I'd lived the life and was confident that I could make that happen, too.

The space was generous. Johnson had created a restaurant big enough for two kitchens. I knew we had to have a kitchen that could do casual food. You have to offer burgers and breakfast in a hotel. I had understood this at the Drake, that I couldn't do Outhier's food in the same kitchen that served the hotel and the Swiss Café, and so I recognized that I would need a second kitchen here as well. I could put a big kitchen and prep area downstairs, along with all the walk-in space. This kitchen would do the bulk of the food. For my four-star restaurant, I would need a four-star kitchen. Again, I wanted it upstairs and on view and open, so that my chefs could be seen.

But the space turned out to be too big. I didn't want to have a 120-seat restaurant. That would be too difficult for the quality that I intended for my gem. What else to do then but open a second, more casual restaurant next to it?

As with the people who ran the Drake back in 1986, the GM's people thought I was crazy. "What?" they said. "You want to have two kitchens and two restaurants *and* serve the hotel?"

I said, "Yes, *I know how to do this*."

In the end, we convinced them. General Electric chose *us*. And I thought, "Wow, here we go."

*

AGAIN, I HAD SAID YES, and it was a yes to my roots in this profession. For nearly twenty years, I'd worked in the highest possible echelons of the food world, the Michelin three-star French restaurants. This was what was in my blood. I had left it in order to branch out on my own, opening a more casual bistro with paper, not white cloth, covering the tables. The next thing I opened was the Lipstick Café, which was part of the requirement for opening Vong. I could have continued to do more casual establishments like that. I could have opened a slew of Vongs and focused on my interpretation of Southeast Asian cuisine, and then sold the concept of a high-end chain to a company that would grow it, which was a movement beginning to happen then.

To all these ideas, I said no. Fine dining was my love; I'd understood that the night I first ate at Auberge de l'Ill on my sixteenth birthday. And I wanted back in.

Poached Foie Gras with Fennel and Caramel– Black Pepper Sauce

I missed foie gras. Monsieur Paul had taught me all the nuances of this very special and specially treated ingredient. But it wasn't something I wanted to put on the menu at JoJo, because the price was too high. I was on my own and needed to keep a close hold on expenses. Throughout my life, I had eaten foie gras only at the holidays, when my *maman* made pounds of it as gifts. Part of what makes the dish so special is the versatility of fattened duck liver. The varieties of preparations are endless. And I wanted to do something fun with it.

When I first came to the United States, fresh foie gras was hardly ever available. And then two Gascons, Jean-Louis Palladin, who had found a way to get it in, and Ariane Daguin, began making it widely available here. Gascony was the original home of foie gras. And a four-star restaurant in New York was *expected* to offer it. This became one of my favorite dishes from the year I opened Jean-Georges. I think I made every single one during the restaurant's first year, which means I've cooked this dish more than ten thousand times, and still I never get tired of making it. I'm not smarter than anyone else. I do surround myself with people smarter than I am—an important thing to do. But I'm good at what I do in part because I make the same dish over and over; excellence is often simply a matter of repetition.

This dish is simple to prepare, but the flavors are complex and powerful because of the intensity of the ingredients, which cover the full range of our taste spectrum: sweet, bitter, acidic, spicy, and fatty. The caramel, which I bring almost to a bitter brown, contrasts with a very sharp pepperiness, and then the sweetness of the fat-enriched, reduced wine, the acidity of the lemon, and the deep richness of the foie gras itself, set against the fresh, delicate licorice perfume of the fennel—the combination is perfect. When I first started working on this dish, I used a Sauternes, the classic pairing with foie gras. But again, I wanted the new, so I chose a Coteaux du Layon from the Loire Valley, 100 percent chenin blanc, an underappreciated grape. But any of the late-harvest or Sauternes-style wines will work.

1 fennel bulb, white section only, fronds reserved for garnish (very important)
1 tablespoon unsalted butter
Salt and freshly ground black pepper to taste

Slice the fennel into 1/2-inch pieces across the grain, or widthwise, which will ensure tenderness without overcooking this sweet, anise-flavored vegetable. Put

it in a small saucepan with water just to cover—you
don't want too much water; you want to keep the
fennel flavor in the water intense, not let it become
diffuse—then add the butter and some salt and pepper for seasoning. Simmer it until it is completely tender but still has body, for five or ten minutes, then set
it aside, uncovered.

> 1½ cups Coteaux du Layon, Sauternes, or
>   other wine of that style
> 2 thick slices of foie gras (½ to ¾ inch thick)

Bring the wine just to a simmer, then add the foie gras
and turn the heat to low. The wine should be hot but
not at a simmer. The foie doesn't need to cook so
much as heat through. If you cook it too hard, it will
release too much fat.

> 4 tablespoons sugar
> 1 teaspoon coarsely chopped black pepper

In a separate pan, over medium heat, add the sugar.
When it begins to melt around the edges, give the
pan a gentle shake to facilitate even melting. When
the sugar is fluid, add the black pepper and continue
to cook the caramel until it is a dark brown. This
will take a few minutes, long enough for the foie gras
just to heat through. Pour about half the wine from
the cooking pot into the caramel, whisking carefully
(the steam will make the caramel bubble violently),
and set the foie gras aside, off the heat. Reduce the

caramel sauce until you have about a quarter cup of sauce, or a couple tablespoons per portion.

Lemon juice as needed for seasoning, 1, 2,
maybe 3 teaspoons

Season the sauce with a healthy squeeze of lemon (taste, think, respond).

Fleur de sel or Maldon salt for finishing

Serve immediately: Spoon a small mound of fennel into the center of a small plate, and repeat this for a second plate. Place a slice of foie gras onto each fennel mound. Poached foie gras isn't pretty, just gray, so it's important to sauce and garnish it thoughtfully. Spoon the pepper-speckled sauce over each piece of foie gras, then garnish with finishing salt, followed by the bright green fennel fronds.

SERVES 2

20.

MAKE IT NEW

ALL ALONG, I HAD A PLAN, HAD BEEN DEVISING IT EVER
since I had first seen Phillip Johnson's drawings. The
downstairs kitchen would not only serve the hotel but
also cook and serve the food for a casual restaurant that
I would call Nougatine (named after a confection I had
first learned to make as a teenager at Auberge). The open
kitchen, a concept I had introduced at Lafayette (we could
actually see when Bryan Miller came in!), would produce
the food for my gem, Jean-Georges. Jean-Georges would
have no more than sixty-five seats and be physically separate from Nougatine. I chose Adam Tihany to design what
was in fact four public spaces: the open kitchen, the bar,
the casual restaurant, and what I was determined would
be a four-star dining room.

This was an extraordinary undertaking, so I would
need to be methodical in my strategy. We would first put
the downstairs kitchen into gear, serving the hotel and
then Nougatine. This would allow us to get the kinks out
of the service and the running of food and give us time to
develop a sense of what we would need to do to manage

the hotel's food. Working a hotel and two restaurants is hard: you're in the middle of lunch service and then the king of Saudi Arabia asks for eggs Benedict. (There were 158 condos and 167 hotel rooms in Trump International Hotel and Tower; all the condos sold and, amazingly, on the first day it opened, so did every hotel room, all but unheard of.)

In the fall of 1996, while continuing to manage JoJo, Lipstick, Vong New York, and Vong London, I began to write the menus for Nougatine and Jean-Georges. We opened Nougatine first, in January 1997. The space for Jean-Georges was finished, but it wasn't time to open. I wanted to get Nougatine on the map first. In the beginning, it had only forty seats, with the front serving mainly as a lounge area for the bar. But everybody wanted to be up front, to be seen, so we would eventually turn that into a dining space as well. Again, always watch the customers, see how they act, listen to what they request. Take these things into account during your decision-making.

All the while, I was working on the food for Jean-Georges. From the beginning—really since that Gael Greene review that had put me in bed for three days—I had focused on how to distinguish my food from that of all the other ambitious chefs in Manhattan. Everyone was upping the game in New York—which is why it was, and still is, such a phenomenal restaurant city. In New York, you can't just do what you've always done. You have to make it new. But in 1997, what was new?

I spent a lot of time reading about plants. One of the authors I read was François Couplan, a Frenchman living in Switzerland. I knew he worked with Michel Bras,

Marc Veyrat, and other Michelin three-star chefs. I convinced Couplan to come to the United States to help me understand edible wild plants. This, I sensed, was unexplored territory in American restaurants. This was new. And so he trained me and he trained the farmer I'd been working with for years, Nancy MacNamara, whose parents owned Jaxberry Farm in Marlboro, New York, south of Poughkeepsie in the Hudson Valley. I'd met her—and this is important—only because some guy had walked into Lafayette in the mid-1980s with late-harvest raspberries he hadn't been able to sell at the green market. He helped me start working with Nancy, so that Jaxberry Farm would begin to grow certain produce specifically for me.

Couplan told us that this area of North America was one of the most diverse spots for wild edibles on the planet. For millennia, it had given native Americans both nutrition and medicine and had been an important part of the native peoples' collective knowledge over all that time. We understood little of this anymore. There were twenty-five hundred edible species here, he explained, and people didn't know a quarter of them. Couplan was passionate about his work, believed that one's relationship with plants was a direct relationship with God. I admired that kind of depth and devotion.

Equally passionate about her farming, Nancy got Couplan to teach her about the many types of "weeds" and ground covers I wanted to serve in my fancy New York restaurant. I was intrigued by the bright citrus flavor of wood sorrel, the earthiness of mugwort, and the root beer/camphor aromatics of sassafras. He showed us lemony ground ivy, nettles, chickweed, yarrow, amaranth, lamb's-quarters, miner's lettuce, dandelions, and Queen Anne's lace, which has a white, carrot-flavored root and whose seeds, which develop from its lacy flower, taste of pears, perfect for sprinkling over a crème brûlée or fruit salad. I would thread these foraged plants through my new menu, whether in a salad of mixed wild greens to go with an earthy porcini tart or by adding mustard garlic, a plant that tastes like both, to the bread crumb coating for lamb chops. (I'm proud to have worked lamb brains into that crust as well—delicious.)

Other dishes sprang into being. One day in the kitchen I had just eaten some raisins when, by chance, I tasted some capers. I noted the way the brininess of the capers paired with the dense sweetness of the raisins. This combination, I thought, would work beautifully in a sauce! So, thanks to a random tasting of two opposing ingredients, I developed the caper-raisin emulsion for seared scallops, a dish still on the menu twenty years later. And it's nothing more complex than that: capers and raisins, plumped with some water, blended, and seasoned with nutmeg.

I would pair squab with Chinese five-spice powder; this dish, like the scallops, is still on the menu today.

I created the elegant and simple foie gras dish I described earlier, a slab of foie poached in what we commonly drink with foie gras dishes, Sauternes. I would pour the poaching liquid into some peppery caramel that I'd make *à la minute*—the Sauternes, now enriched with rendered foie fat, combines beautifully with the bittersweet caramel and spicy pepper as it reduces to a syrup, all served on poached fennel, which I love for its freshness and licorice notes, to contrast with the rich foie.

After almost three months of running Nougatine, and with the final menu written and all the dishes tested, I was ready to pull the trigger on Jean-Georges. We opened on March 17, 1997, the day after my fortieth birthday. But we opened slowly. I knew that I had to be *very* careful. With my sights set on four stars, I couldn't risk a single mistake. So I took my time. I allowed only twenty covers for lunch, forty for dinner. I didn't care about the money. That would come if we got those four stars. After a week or so, with the reservation book kept half empty, and a long list of names on the waiting list begging for a table, my team was asking me to do more covers, let more people in, saying, We're going to lose money. And my servers wanted to earn more. They were making only half what they might have been if we worked at capacity.

I said, "Just wait, wait for the review. First, make it perfect—the money comes after. Don't worry. Wait for that review."

With just sixty covers each weekday, and forty covers on Saturdays (we didn't serve lunch on Saturday), I could practically cook everyone's meal myself. I had a great team in the kitchen, but I also had my hand on every dish that left it. I tasted every single dish before it went out. I cooked every service, which gave me Saturday mornings free, and all day Sunday to rest. I talk a lot about how a chef inevitably loses 10, 15, 20 percent of himself in the brigade's translation of his or her food. But that first year of Jean-Georges, it was the closest I could come to closing that gap. I cooked every single Sauternes-poached foie that went out, made every caramel–black pepper sauce for it *à la minute*—for a *year*.

I imagined new food and new, contemporary ways of serving it, but I also didn't forget my roots. Never forget your roots. The menu for Jean-Georges was 100 percent my DNA. I served a garlic soup that was essentially the same soup my mother made my whole life, but I refined it and served it with frogs' legs.

And more. The garlic soup is so seductive when your face is over the pan on the stove, the steam wafting up—such a pleasure. I talk about this a lot in the recipes in this book. I take so much pleasure in those moments of cooking. But this wasn't enough. I wanted the *diner* to have this experience, the experience of the cook, to inhale that heady aroma. So I decided to serve only some chive blossoms in a beautiful bowl. Our servers would pour the soup tableside, so that the aroma would be released as it hit the warm bowl and the chive flowers. Then the frogs' legs, delicately crispy and hot, would be set down to complete the dish. It harkened back to the tableside service I'd been so much a part of in the 1970s and '80s.

I was intent on being completely original, while keeping in mind my often difficult audience: New Yorkers who want five four-star courses but need to get out in under two hours. If that's what they want, I resolved, we can do that. I've never been a prima donna that way—I always listen to my customers and try to give them what they desire. You must always listen.

I wanted the servers to be refined but casual, to make the guests feel comfortable and at ease. The days of intimidating French service, I knew, were finished. So I took the servers out of their tuxedos and put them in more contemporary suits and vests. I installed, as far as I know, the first female captain ever of a formal French dining room in Manhattan. I trained a mixed-sex staff of servers as well.

I took the spinach-like lamb's quarters Nancy harvested and made a soup of it, with fresh, sweet crab to counter the slight, pleasing bitterness of the leaf. I would dust sweetbreads with powder made from dehydrated mango, serve them with carrot and ginger, that wonderful pairing, along with a splash of white port and a hint of licorice. I wanted my flavors to astonish. I wanted New Yorkers' imaginations to explode from the intensity. I wanted everyone to feel the wonder and amazement I'd felt that first morning when I set foot in Thailand seventeen years earlier, tasted my first bowl of tom yum kung. This excitement and revelation is still available to us. That was my benchmark for the power of flavor—street food in Bangkok. And I wanted to serve it within the seductive luxury of a four-star restaurant in Manhattan looking out into Central Park.

As the first month moved into the second, my people worried. "We're only doing forty covers—we need to do more," they kept reminding me. No, I continued to tell them, wait, concentrate on perfecting the food and the service. It takes weeks to iron everything out. *Be patient, stay focused, do your job.* This should be your daily mantra.

*

ON JUNE 6, 1997, the review came—from Ruth Reichl, one of the most important voices and writers in the food world, then and now. As restaurant critic for the *New York Times*, she opened her review with these words:

> It is tempting to abandon yourself to the sensual pleasure of the place, sink into the comfortable seats and allow the staff to surround you with aroma and seduce you with flavor. But take a deeper look: in his quiet way the chef and co-owner, Jean-Georges Vongerichten, is creating a restaurant revolution. This is an entirely new kind of four-star restaurant.

We'd done it.

We. My whole team, at JoJo, at the café, at Vong, at Vong London. None of this would have been possible had I not built a team. It was one team. And we'd done it.

Sea Bass with Seeds and Nuts

This dish originated from memories of a 1983 trip I took to Goa. I loved, loved to travel. Instead of going home on my breaks from the restaurant in Bangkok, I would travel—to Vietnam, Cambodia, and Laos. Goa is a state in the middle of the western coast of India, on the Arabian Sea, so the locals cook a lot of seafood. Much of it, when I was there, they crusted in nuts and seeds or fried in ghee, browned clarified butter. The smells were amazing. I'll never forget them. They also served their fish with all kinds of sweet-and-sour sauces, very powerfully flavored. This was my inspiration in creating this dish. But it could not simply duplicate the street food of Goa. This would be for the opening menu of Jean-Georges, which I was determined would have four *New York Times* stars. This is one of the more complex dishes in this book; there's a lot going on here—nuts and spices, a sweet-and-sour sauce, a diverse garnish—which is the kind of cooking one expects from a four-star restaurant.

For the sauce, I went back in my mind to my Outhier days. I would make a water-based sauce—in fact, a quick mushroom broth. Mushrooms have such amazing depth of flavor if you coax it out of them. We don't do a fish fumet at the restaurant—we only make chicken stock. I find you don't need fumet. So mushrooms and water are the base for this fish dish. I cook the mushrooms hard, then simmer them so that all their flavor goes into the sauce. And cheap mushrooms, too. You wouldn't want to use expensive cèpes here. Mushrooms and water are the base for a very pungent sweet-and-sour sauce that I consider tart enough to work as a vinaigrette, balanced with honey. It's all about balance. This sauce has seven ingredients, but it teaches so many lessons in creating extraordinary complexity.

I start the sauce by cooking thinly sliced mushrooms in some butter.

1 pound inexpensive mushrooms, thinly sliced
2 tablespoons unsalted butter

Put the mushrooms and butter into a large sauté pan over medium-high heat. They should be sliced thinly because you want as much surface area to brown as possible. You're looking for a deep brown caramelized color. They will cook and cook, releasing their water, which evaporates, leaving the sugars from the vegetable to caramelize in the pan. This takes a good twenty minutes or so of sautéing them, jumping them in the pan so that they cook evenly.

2 tablespoons honey

When the mushrooms are cooked down about as far as they'll go and there's a nice brown fond in the pan, I add the honey. I stir the mushrooms, mixing the honey around as it thins in the heat so that they become coated. This will turn everything a dark chestnut brown and caramelize further, becoming increasingly complex. Smell the pan—the aroma will be earthy and rich and sweet. Once I have the color I want, a mellow dark, rich brown, I add the remaining ingredients for the sauce—or, really, the sauce base, since I intend to cook cherry tomatoes in it to finish the sauce.

1½ cups water

As I'm stirring the mushrooms and honey, I add the magic ingredient: water—about a cup and a half. The water will pull all the umami flavors from the mushrooms, dissolve the fond in the pan, and bring all the flavors together. That's the sauce base. Mushrooms cooked down, down, down, then honey for more caramelization and sweet complexity, then water.

> 2 tablespoons Banyuls vinegar or sherry
>   vinegar
> 2 tablespoons lemon juice
> 2 tablespoons soy sauce

For flavor and sharpness, I next swirl in the acid: vinegar and lemon. Notice that I use twice as much acid as honey. Then, finally, more umami and salt in the form of soy sauce. I still keep the mushrooms in the pot, to extract more flavor.

By the time the water has pulled everything out, the mushrooms have no flavor. At home we would serve these—we wouldn't throw them out. At the restaurant, I strain this sauce through a chinois into a saucepan, pressing on the mushrooms to extract as much liquid as possible. Taste the sauce. It should have a distinct and powerful sweet-and-sour profile, too strong to enjoy on its own.

While this reduces—not too much, just a very, very light cooking—I get the seeds and nuts toasting. They will become the crust for the fish.

½ tablespoon black peppercorns
1 tablespoon whole coriander
1 tablespoon sesame seeds
2 hazelnuts
2 almonds

Put all of these in a small sauté pan over medium heat and toast them until they smell fragrant, a couple of minutes. (More flavor will be released when they cook on the fish.) Then grind them in a mortar or in a spice grinder. I like to leave them a little rough, not too fine, so that when you bite into them you taste the distinct flavors of each, the coriander, the nuts.

4 sea bass fillets, skin on
Salt
Cayenne
A little cream, as needed
Flour as needed
Oil for sautéing as needed

Black sea bass is one of my favorite fish, and they're caught right here off the coast of New York. Season the flesh side with salt and a fine dusting of cayenne. Turn the fillets over and paint the skin side with cream so that the crust will adhere. Press the crust mixture onto the fish. You want a good uniform coating. Give the crust a light dusting of flour. This will help to protect the seeds from scorching against the direct heat of the steel.

2 cups of a variety of cherry tomatoes, some
  halved, others left whole
¼ cup fingerling potatoes cut in half-inch
  disks, blanched till tender and set aside
¼ cup peeled fava beans, blanched and
  shocked
¼ cup mushrooms, cut into small pieces
¼ cup pearl onions, peeled, shocked, and
  blanched

Add the tomatoes, potatoes, favas, mushrooms, and pearl onions to the sauce. They'll need to cook very lightly, just till warmed through. A minute or three, depending on the temperature. Taste a tomato, and if it is delightfully soft and bursts pleasantly and tenderly in the mouth, take the pan off the heat while you finish the fish. Notice how perfectly they enhance the sauce and how they give the sauce just the right balance of sweetness and acidity.

In a hot sauté pan (at the restaurant we cook them on a *plancha*), with a little oil, lay the fish crust side down, and press down on each fillet firmly with a spatula to establish a good crisp crust. You can be fairly aggressive here. Once a crust has formed and the spices have toasted further, sixty seconds or so, turn the fish to cook them briefly on the flesh side. They need only a little cooking—just enough to warm the center. Remove them to a rack or a paper-towel-lined plate to rest briefly.

To serve, divide the sauce and vegetables among four bowls. Rest the fillets on the tomatoes.

1 tablespoon chopped tarragon
1 tablespoon mint chiffonade

Garnish each bowl with tarragon and mint and serve.

SERVES 4

21.

LEARN FROM FAILURE

I'VE OPENED MORE THAN SEVENTY RESTAURANTS. I CUR-
rently have nearly forty. That means that some I've opened
have closed. Most have closed because they lived out their
life or we chose not to renew the lease. Vong, for example, we closed in 2011 (though, frankly, I'd love to bring
Vong back). The rent had quadrupled, and after twenty
years, the dining room and kitchen needed a substantial
upgrade, likely more than $1 million worth of work. It
didn't make financial sense.

Other restaurants, ones we license and open in hotels,
sometimes don't succeed because the hotel's leadership
brings the restaurant down. Chambers Kitchen, in the
Chambers Hotel in Minneapolis, which opened in
2006, is a good example. It did well, but then new manag-
ers began changing design elements within the restaurant
and the way front of the house was run. When new people
arrive, they have to change things, to put their stamp on
it. We typically sign ten-year contracts for licensing deals,
with extensions, meaning we have the option to extend

the lease if we want to. In this case, the partnership didn't work and we decided not to renew the contract.

But we learned from this. Now we write into the contracts that no changes can be made to the restaurant without our approval, and this has had a positive impact on those restaurants that my team doesn't directly manage.

If you don't learn from your failures, you're bound to repeat them. I've had mainly successes, but I've had two big flops in New York City. This is always hard.

When the Time Warner Center opened on Columbus Circle in 2004, we were part of a collection of very high-end groups asked to put a restaurant into what is in effect a New York City mall, a collection that included Masa Takayama, Thomas Keller, and Gray Kunz, all of them *New York Times* four-star chefs.

I already had my four-star gem across the street, so I didn't want to do a four-star concept there. I wanted to do something familiar but new. Make it new, right?

Big mistake!

I thought it was a great idea at the time: a reimagined steak house. We took all the staples of a classic American steak house and deconstructed them. We reinvented the Caesar salad. We took apart the clam chowder.

But the diners didn't want to combine the potatoes and clams and broth themselves. They didn't want to make their own French onion soup by dipping croutons in cheese, then sipping onion broth. Everybody *hated* it.

Including Frank Bruni, the *New York Times*' restaurant critic at the time. In a piece for Diner's Journal, a column that offered prereview coverage, among other news, he wrote, "When a celebrity chef branches out as far as

Jean-Georges has, this is where he winds up: on the prec-
ipice of parody, confident that an educated public will follow him there."

Guess what. Nobody followed me!

I thought it was delicious. Everything. I swear to God, it
was so tasty. There was no reason to kill V Steakhouse, but
it happened. What I didn't realize was, Americans want
some things always to be the same. One of those things is
their steak house. This is an American institution and is
not to be messed with (and our eventual steak houses, two
of them, in Las Vegas bear this out).

We took a risk, but we could afford to because we didn't
spend a dime on the place. The company in charge of the
Time Warner Center, they built it and more or less gave us
the keys. After two years, we gave the keys back. We had
said, "You know, let's do a crazy steak house!" It didn't
work, even though we were doing $10 million in annual
sales. The reviews killed us. And I was the only one who
liked the food. Even my *partner,* Phil Suarez, didn't like it.

The restaurant was not doomed because it was in a New
York City mall (Per Se and Masa are thriving there to this
day). The fabulous, ornate design and comfortable tables
and fabulous service weren't enough to save it. Even millions in sales wasn't enough to make it worthwhile. The
bottom line was that no one liked the food. Again: listen
to the customer.

*

MY OTHER FLOP was our Chinese restaurant called 66.

I maintain to this day that 66 served the best Chinese
food in the city. I'd traveled all over China, gathering

ideas, starting with my first years in Bangkok. Whenever I go anywhere, I come back with twenty or thirty new recipes or ideas. And the whole time I'd traveled around China and Asia, I'd made a point of collecting. I love Chinese food for its complexity, and for how utterly different it is from Western cuisines. Looking back on it, there was one Chinese restaurant near where I'd grown up, run by a Chinese immigrant: La Rivière des Parfums. It was okay—Chinese-Alsatian was about as exotic as it got for me there. The chef surely had trouble locating ingredients and must have had to make do with what he could find in France and Germany.

So later, working from my travels and with my team, I created a fabulous menu for 66. The restaurant was in Tribeca, a difficult location way downtown, but still we were busy. The place was very hard to get into. It was filled with celebrities. There were thousands of Chinese restaurants in the city, though relatively few authentic ones outside Chinatown and fewer that served innovative food based on the Chinese traditions I'd learned during my years in Asia.

Unfortunately, then we had an incident. The editor of a big, influential magazine, whom I won't name, arrived one evening and demanded a table. This was a time when you could still smoke in restaurants, so all restaurants had to have a smoking section. Well, for this editor, who had arrived with no reservation and was giving the manager a very hard time about getting him a table, we could only squeeze him and his party into a table in the nonsmoking section. But this editor insisted on smoking. Customers complained. We eventually had to tell him that we couldn't serve him and had to escort him out of the restaurant.

It was a real scene, and the editor didn't leave happy!

Worse, he then sent a British journalist in to review the restaurant. The guy was little more than a hit man, assigned to trash the restaurant for the editor's magazine. (And this was a magazine that didn't even run restaurant reviews—usually not more than a couple hundred words, anyway.) Our customers were his demographic, a high-end, society-minded crowd. In August 2003, the article came out. The editor and the writer hammered the first nail in the coffin, for sure. All because we'd asked him to put out his cigarette.

But the location had to have something to do with it, as well. One review in that kind of magazine can't torpedo a business. Ours was an expensive Chinese restaurant blocks away from Chinatown, filled with inexpensive Chinese restaurants—that couldn't have helped. In Manhattan in 2008, 2009, Tribeca was still a long way downtown for many New Yorkers. And if there was any doubt that the location hurt it, that was put to rest when I changed the concept. I brought in a Japanese restaurateur to open a soba noodle restaurant in the same space, and that only lasted three years.

Location has a major impact on business. I should have listened to my feng shui advisor, Jerome (who had similarly tried to discourage me from opening the Time Warner steak house). After eight years, I knew to cut our losses. So we closed it down. *C'est la vie.* Move on. Never look back.

*

I HAVE ALSO BEEN personally attacked in print by a journalist, someone we thought was a friend, who had always glowingly reviewed us. You have to be tough, you have to get over it and move forward, but at the time it was a blow to me and to my team.

It happened in the mid-2000s, a time when many chefs were expanding. Vegas, which had begun luring chefs in big numbers, represented a concentrated example of this. There was plenty of talk in the air among chefs about having an "exit strategy" and how to make a lot of money. And the critics seemed to resent it when chefs expanded. Some of them seemed to believe that the executive chef personally prepares every dish for every customer. In fact, the mark of a great chef is when he doesn't have to prepare each dish, when he and his staff are so perfectly aligned that the dishes are not distinguishable as the work of one or the other or they have reduced that 10 to 20 percent distance I spoke of earlier. Granted, we had a lot going on, and we were admittedly spreading ourselves thin. We had just opened Spice Market in the Meatpacking District of Manhattan—at the time, a dead zone, although now a hotbed. It immediately received three stars, and suddenly we went from doing three hundred covers a day to one thousand. This journalist used me as an example, saying basically that I was absent from the stove. It was so ruthless, so gratuitously mean, I stayed in bed for two days.

But then I got out of bed, and I gathered my staff. They felt terrible, as if they had personally let me down. Of course, the problem was not them. We sat down and evaluated the situation. What could we be doing better? We tried to learn from the criticism, as I had from Gael Greene. I always listen to criticism, even when it stings so personally.

Two years later, this same journalist walked in to Jean-Georges and took a seat at the bar. I was surprised that he'd show his face. My chef de cuisine wanted to throw him out. But I told my chef, That's not what we do. He's a customer, and we treat him like a customer. So we sent some food out to him, compliments of the kitchen. Even he was surprised, and ultimately this journalist wrote me a letter that was in effect an apology.

Again, this industry is too small. Be good to people, even those who are mean to you. Turn them around. Grudges won't do you any good.

*

MOST RECENTLY, while I was writing this book, my team took another blow. For twelve years, every year since Michelin had begun publishing a guide to restaurants in New York City, Jean-Georges had been awarded three Michelin stars, the highest accolade from the European critics and the system I'd grown up with. In October 2017, I got a call, as I usually do, from the then head, Michael Ellis. But it came on a Sunday. For the previous dozen years, the call had come on a Monday morning, the day of the announcements. He said they'd been in three times, and things hadn't been as sharp. I asked for examples. He repeated that things hadn't been sharp. A squab dish had bled into the sauce a little. I don't care if it's not Instagrammable, I said, how did it taste? (Instagram, I feel, is harmful in that way. People want pretty over taste, and that's not a good thing. On the other hand, I love Instagram—it is a great way of sharing food information that we couldn't have conceived of when I was a young cook.)

The next day it was announced that we'd lost a Michelin star. Michael tried to tell me that our Brazil restaurant (open for only ten months) had gotten a star, and so had our restaurant in Shanghai. So, I asked him, I'm supposed to be happy? You take a star from Jean-Georges to give it to Shanghai?

I was angry and upset. But most of all, I was worried about my staff. That's the kind of setback that can make them feel as if they've personally let me down, and that's the last thing I want. They work hard. They care about their work. They're my team. *We* are a team.

It was true that we'd had a busy year. We'd pushed ourselves. We'd opened five restaurants that year, in four countries. And we had done a major renovation of my beloved first restaurant, JoJo. Five restaurants in a year, and millions in renovations. Ask any chef and they'll tell you that's not easy. Especially when it involves Michelin-starred restaurants. I'd had key members of my team—Greg and Danny especially, mainstays at Jean-Georges—on the road continually. So yes, it's totally possible that we weren't up to snap.

So I sat down with my staff. We discussed it. I said, Relax. Then *snap out of it and get back to work*. It's not terrible, I told them. (Terrible would be losing a *New York Times* star; that would be hard.) Ultimately, I said, it's a good thing. It will force us to look at our dishes, our service, recalibrate recipes, sharpen *everything*. It's easier to lose a star than to get one back, but that's our goal. And next year, I hope to get that call. On Monday morning, and not on Sunday!

*

HERE'S A STORY that matters to me more than any Michelin star.

We can never forget the business we are in, yes? We are not here so that we can be praised. We're not in this business to get stars, grateful as we are for them. We are here to serve people. We're here to make people feel good. That's what the business is all about.

Because of this, you must become very good at reading people. You must always be looking, seeing, questioning. This man, this woman, this couple, this eight-top—are they enjoying themselves? Do they like the food? Are they comfortable and at ease? Do they have everything they need? Are they happy?

Not long ago, I was at the pass of the open Jean-Georges kitchen, where I can see the bar and all the tables in Nougatine. At the far end were two ladies. The restaurant was very busy because it was restaurant week, when we offer menus at a fraction of the normal price. A lot of chefs groan about it, but I *love* restaurant week. It's a win for all. It gives us a chance to cook for and serve people who wouldn't ordinarily dine with us. If they like it, they tell people. And we hope they like it so much that they come back. It takes place twice a year, in deepest winter and midsummer, both times when restaurants tend to be less busy. So we're not losing money by discounting meals. It's a win for everyone. I love it.

That afternoon during restaurant week, I watched these two ladies enjoy their lunch. And they really were enjoying themselves, talking, laughing, sharing their food. That's always a good sign, to see people sharing. I try to watch every table. This time, I sensed that this was a special experience for them. I'm not sure what it was—their ages, their dress—but I just got the feeling that they weren't the sort to go often to a restaurant like Nougatine. And then I noticed that they even had a dessert wine, which is something people do only when they want to extend a meal, which they only do if they're happy.

But when I looked over at them again as they were finishing up, their mood had changed. I could see the change from all the way across the room. The laughter was gone. The smiles were gone. They were clearly subdued and had sour expressions. This is not how it typically progresses. We want to make sure that the mood of a good meal follows them out of the restaurant and stays with them. But they were no longer happy.

What had happened?

When they'd gone, I asked their server how the women had liked their meal. He told me they'd loved it. I asked him, What happened?

He looked at me perplexed and said, "What do you mean?"

I said, "Something happened."

The server shook his head and shrugged.

I left it at that.

A few days later, I received a letter from a female customer, and I knew as soon as I read it exactly who it was—

one of the women at the table, describing their meal. Now I understood what had happened.

They had, as I'd seen, had a great meal, and she thanked me for that. But after the meal, she wrote, their server talked them into a dessert wine to conclude the experience. They were having such a good time, they said sure. But it was an expensive Château d'Yquem, and they hadn't been made aware of the cost, had simply trusted the server. When their bill came, they saw that the two dessert wines cost more than the entire meal. They spent sixty dollars on lunch and eighty dollars on wine they didn't need. As they'd obviously come to the restaurant because cost was an issue for them, this was upsetting. And so they left feeling sour.

My server really had no idea what had happened. It's probably needless to say that he didn't stay with us much longer. Not because of this incident. I spoke with him about it. But it was, in fact, his inability to *see* the customer that doomed him as a server. You have to be able to read people. You have to make them want to come back. It's up to you, personally, each one of you, each cook, each server, each back waiter.

I immediately invited the woman back to the restaurant for a complimentary meal. It should be obvious, but perhaps it's not: no one, ever, should leave your restaurant angry. Ever. All my servers are instructed to make the situation right immediately if they sense that anyone is unhappy—people should only go home happy. But these women had clearly left my restaurant upset, and it had been up to me to turn it around. Think about it. Had I not reached out to her, these two women would have forever spoken badly of the restaurant. It was too pricey, they'd say, the service wasn't good, simply because they'd left it unhappily. And they might tell a hundred people over the course of a couple of years. So it was prudent to try to make them feel good again. But also, frankly, I simply wanted these two women, just as they were, to leave my restaurant happy.

It should be common sense that you want everyone to leave feeling great, and if you can't detect a negative feeling, you can't change it. I've never left a job on bad terms when I could help it—at Bocuse it was close, but Chef Paul was a gracious man. As I've said, in business, always leave on good terms—you don't want any bad blood with colleagues, chefs, or servers. This is a good rule generally in business, but it's especially important in the restaurant and hospitality world. And you should feel the same about your customer—ensure that they leave on good terms, which means happy, sated, and pleased with the meal and the service they've just experienced. Otherwise they won't come back. And if they don't want to come back, they certainly won't encourage others to try the restaurant. Also, ours is such an insular community, you're bound to be thrown into circumstances down the line with that very person you pissed off. Or that journalist.

*

THIS WAS HOW we would continue to grow, by serving customers and making them happy. We opened a restaurant right below where I live, called Perry St.; it is run by my son, Cédric, a graduate of the Culinary Institute of Amer-

ica. We opened a restaurant focused on all the fresh vegetables and meat a few blocks away at the Union Square
Greenmarket. Since it was in the building that housed one
of New York's most famous stores, ABC Carpet & Home,
I called the restaurant ABC Kitchen—that way, everyone
would know exactly where it was! When the space next
to it became available, we decided to do a Spanish-style
restaurant, ABC Cocina. One of the dishes there, the pea
guacamole, was so controversial, even the president of the
United States weighed in on it! We were having fun. And
most recently, right next to Cocina, we began building
a totally vegetarian restaurant. We've opened in several
hotels, and we've even opened a spot in Madison Square
Garden. What to look for next in New York? I'm aching to
get back to my Thai roots, where I truly came of age and
which gave me the creativity to get where I am today.

#Givepeasachance Guacamole

Here's one of our favorite recipes from ABC Cocina. I
love it, first because it was another departure for me,
reimagining a classic preparation, and also because
of controversy that went all the way to the White
House. It began when we created the ABC Cocina
menu, our take on Mexican and Latin food. We
had to have guacamole on the menu because people
would expect it. But we couldn't do a straightforward

guacamole—that's not who we are. In New York City, I've learned, you have to surprise people. My customers would be expecting something new from me. It was our director of culinary development, chef Greg Brainin, who suggested the peas, and even this was somewhat happenstance. The restaurant had been scheduled to open in the fall, but by the time it actually opened, it was spring and peas were in full flourish. So peas it was!

What would happen, Greg wondered, if we mixed chopped peas with avocado? And soon we had a very fresh, sweet, super-green dish. The color was amazing. We enhanced the peas with cilantro and roasted jalapeños (charred and peeled, but we used the whole pepper, seeds and all, because jalapeños have become so mild, and I wanted the seeds for some spice). We finished the dish with sunflower seeds because I love sunflower seeds and knew their salty crunch would be a great and uncommon addition to the customary garnishes we use, baby cilantro, scallion, and minced jalapeño.

We were working with Latin American flavors and ingredients and dishes, and this came uncommonly easy for us. After a while, we realized why: the northern parts of Latin America are at the same latitude as Southeast Asia, which influences so much of our cooking. We said to one another, "We're on the other side of the world, but we know how to cook things that grow at this latitude!"

So we put our neo-guacamole on the menu. Melissa Clark wrote about it in a *New York Times* cooking blog when we first opened in 2013. Two years later, the *Times* tweeted a link, and suddenly the Internet exploded with angry tweets about how you couldn't bastardize guacamole. President Obama weighed via Twitter (he was in the no-pea camp). People created hashtags for it, such as #givepeasachance. The media called it "Peagate," and Eater.com called it the recipe that broke the Internet. I loved the controversy! The president of the United States was commenting on one of our recipes!

I'm not going to give any exact amounts for this recipe because guacamole is so basic; it simply depends on how many you're serving and how many avocados you have. The important ratio to remember is that you want two parts avocado and one part chopped peas. You'll want to use about a half cup of peas, chopped with one roasted jalapeño and a big pinch of cilantro leaves, for each avocado.* Use fresh peas if peas are in season. But frozen peas work fine as well; if they're good peas and properly frozen, they are better than mediocre fresh peas. And it's impossible for me to teach you how to season in a book; the only way to do this is: I season, we taste and discuss. As a rule, season higher with acid (lime juice) and heat (jalapeño) than you think you should. And don't leave out the sunflower seeds.

---

* For anyone who wants to make a larger batch, this is our official pea-mixture ratio for ten portions, or ten avocados: 1,600 grams peas, 400 grams roasted jalapeño, 40 grams cilantro, 24 grams salt.

Combine the following in a food processor:

Peas (fresh or thawed from frozen), blanched
    and shocked
Jalapeños, charred over a gas flame or under a
    broiler, stems and skin removed
Cilantro

Pulse until everything is combined and the peas are coarsely chopped.

Avocado

Put your avocado into a bowl and add half as much pea mixture as you have avocado. Mash and mix to combine.

Lime juice
Salt

Season with lime juice and salt. Taste and taste again, adding more lime and salt as necessary.

Garnish with the following:

Chopped jalapeño
Thinly sliced scallion
Whole peas (blanched and shocked)
Baby cilantro leaves (or cilantro chiffonade)
Sunflower seeds

MAKES 2 PORTIONS FOR EACH AVOCADO

22.

TO GROW,
BUILD A TEAM

WE ARRIVED IN SINGAPORE IN THE WINTER OF 2017 AT
seven a.m., I and the key players of my team—my brother
Philippe, Sean Considine, Danny Del Vecchio—to open a
new restaurant, the Dempsey Cookhouse. In a city where
I had opened for Outhier in the 1980s. Greg Brainin and
Thomas McKenna, two of my lead chefs, were already
there training the new staff.

My brother Philippe was, of course, our front-of-the-
house maestro.

Daniel Del Vecchio manages all the Jean-Georges
group's restaurants worldwide. Danny came aboard as a
grill cook at Vong and did so well that I sent him to lead
Vong London; today, he's executive vice president of the
company and has become my operations expert in terms
of opening.

Greg Brainin, a philosophy major at the prestigious
Gallatin School at NYU who turned to cooking, is the
man in charge of overseeing flavor—our culinary director
charged with ensuring that the dishes in Singapore will be
exactly as good as they are at my New York restaurants.

Greg grew up in New Jersey in the 1970s, not exactly a culinary mecca at the time. Somehow he developed a palate on his own. "The first thing I learned how to season was my parents' Bloody Marys," he'll tell you. "Lemon, Worcestershire, Tabasco, salt, and pepper. It told me everything I needed to know about seasoning. I was six." I love that.

And, among too many to mention, Sean Considine, pastry wizard—he will get the sweet kitchen up and running.

I have always said that the key to my being a successful leader—I employ more than a thousand people—is first of all, flexibility. You must be flexible. Adapt. Be ready to take advantage of opportunity. Like the pop-up in London.

Like moving from my personally designed luxurious open kitchen at Lafayette to the tiny JoJo kitchen. That was like moving from the Versailles to a food truck. But I did it. I didn't complain, I *adapted*. I was flexible. I looked at where I came from, I looked to my mother. She had cooked for dozens of people every day, three services! Not one. My kitchen at JoJo had *six* burners. How lucky was that! I had two extra burners! I made great sauces using ketchup because we couldn't use those burners for stocks, and I earned three stars for such dishes. Flexibility is key.

The next critical component of leadership is developing your team. I have always surrounded myself with people smarter than me. I'm not that smart—I dropped out of school at sixteen. When I was young, I was a *little* kid, the smallest in my family, like my mom. But I was a leader and so, in the world of kid-dom, I surrounded myself with big guys, people who were stronger than I was. Although I'm an introvert by nature, I know how to gather a team, and more: put those team members in the right place. Gregory Brainin is masterful at creating great dishes. He can handle himself fine at the pass, expediting, running the night's service, though it's not what he's best at. Mark Lapico is *great* at the pass. Utterly unflappable. A calm perfectionist. Daniel Del Vecchio, a super cook, started at Vong, opened Vong London, worked the line at La Côte Basque, one of New York's French landmarks, before he came to me—a great cook, but he's really good at business, at organization, and he loves it. He also created and oversees our full database of thousands of recipes. Who could have predicted that when I was making him cry over the sauce Jacqueline (a very sweet vegetable stock that we would mount with foie fat and finish with a splash of vodka) on the line at Vong? Today he oversees the entire network of worldwide restaurants, checking in on each one personally every week, a total phenom.

You first have to get the right people, and then you have to watch them and make sure they find *their* perfect place. Line cook, prep cook, server, business guy, front of the house, culinary director. This takes time. You have to be patient. But if you watch, you *see*.

We flew to Singapore to join the others already here, who had been hiring and training staff. I needed these guys more than I can say. We were about to open a major restaurant on the other side of the world, one that should be poised to do $8 million in sales in the first year, staffed with young cooks and servers who had virtually no training beyond culinary school, let alone any familiarity with the standards that united my team in New York. And a week ago, I hadn't even had an executive chef. When I touched down on this tiny island off the southern coast of Malaysia, my executive chef, new to our team and hired just days ago, was still not here.

To this day, I love and value the interactions among my chefs. When everyone is in their proper place, your team works in sync. I love the early hours in the kitchen, before service approaches and the restaurant gets busy, hours of prep when we can talk about our pasts and our experiences and dishes we've had and places we've worked. This is an unending source of information and inspiration. It's what we had done every night after service with Eckart Witzigmann. And as I had done for Outhier when I'd returned to him to prepare for Bangkok. He would ask me to make him a dish from Bocuse, such as the *poularde de Bresse en vessie*, dishes from Eckart. This remains one of the best ways of learning.

This kind of communication results in new dishes all the time. Just last week, a chef at Nougatine was married in Korea. He came back and said he'd had a sauce made with the liquid from kimchi, the fermented cabbage preparation ubiquitous there. I said, "Put it on a plate." And he created a dish, pairing it with roasted sea bass and broccoli rabe. It was great. We put it on the menu as "roasted sea bass with red chili sauce," not kimchi sauce, but that's where the idea came from, via one of my chefs. In the same way, I'm not going to call a dish at JoJo "cod with ketchup sauce." But that's what *I* call it. And you, know, it's pretty amazing, that sauce. This is how we develop a repertoire of thousands of great dishes that we can use on menus throughout the world.

Never forget what a great resource your colleagues

are for new dishes and new combinations; tap into their knowledge and experience, and share yours.

*

OPENING A NEW RESTAURANT overseas is a big deal, and this one in Singapore was especially critical, as it was for Christina Ong. The head of the COMO Hotels and Resorts, she is a shrewd businessperson and reportedly one of the wealthiest women in the world, not to mention married to billionaire Ong Beng Seng. I'd met her when the Formula One Grand Prix returned here; during this annual event, we cooked for thousands of people. When she took over what used to be a military barracks in the Dempsey Hill area of Singapore, to create a luxury dining collection, she brought in some of the best in the world.

Ippoh Tempura Bar, whose flagship, Ippoh, in Tokyo, Japan, made some of the finest tempura anywhere and was considered one of the best restaurants in the world, was serving classical Japanese tempura. The other restaurant was Candlenut, which had earned a Michelin star for its Peranakan cuisine, a Malaysian-Chinese blend featuring impressive curries. And the last was to be my restaurant, the Dempsey Cookhouse and Bar. So I understood that ours absolutely had to be good. As I've said, I'm competitive. Our menu would be a kind of greatest hits, the favorite dishes from all my restaurants in New York. This would make opening a little easier, though no part is truly easy. But we were opening with tested-and-true and loved dishes, not dishes that need revision.

This would not be like opening in New York. New York is always about the new, as with the just-opened ABCV, my first venture into a vegetarian menu; it is connected to ABC Kitchen, which focuses on market fare, and ABC Cocina, which offers Spanish fare (but also new dishes, such as the pea guacamole). We had just opened ABCV—*just,* as in *hours* before I'd left for Singapore; Philippe and I had gotten into a town car bound for JFK the very day it opened. This wasn't how I'd planned it, but ABCV had been delayed for weeks, while we waited for new gas lines to be installed in the building. Sometimes you just have to make it all work. Be flexible. The dishes at ABCV are all originals, including new curries, such as *khichri,* a curried breakfast porridge from Rita Chopra, the wife of Deepak Chopra, congee, and other savory breakfast dishes from other parts of the world, but I felt confident in leaving the restaurant in the capable hands of executive chef Neal Harden.

In Singapore, I would be able to combine the egg caviar from Jean-Georges, the pea guacamole from ABC Cocina, the roasted carrots with cumin from ABC Kitchen, the truffle and fontina pizza from Mercer Kitchen, then reach back to the Jean-Georges menu for the Parmesan-crusted chicken with artichoke and lemon-basil sauce (one of my favorite dishes).

So that was the plan for when we reached Singapore— to make sure the young cooks on the line would be able to execute all these familiar dishes.

*

WHEN WE ARRIVED in Singapore after the twenty-hour trip from New York and ABCV's opening day, the first thing Philippe and I did was head to the gym, to clear the travel from our heads and get the blood flowing. We had slept well on the flights—that, plus exercise, followed by a solid breakfast is the way to stay on track when your time zone is twelve hours behind you. After breakfast with my team, I was eager to get to the restaurant—my first time seeing the place—and meet the rest of the team and the new staff. The first of two friends-and-family dinners would begin in nine hours, and opening night would be right on the heels of that.

I was a bit more anxious than usual because of the New York opening hours earlier. The Dempsey Cookhouse and Bar in Singapore would welcome its first dinner guests as the ABCV kitchen in Manhattan began its fifth breakfast service. What's more, we weren't just opening *these* two restaurants back to back. This year, as I've noted, we would inaugurate *five* restaurants on four different continents, including those in Brazil and London, at the Connaught hotel, along with the New York vegetarian restaurant, one in Los Angeles, and another here in Singapore. More in one year than ever before. My opening team would head to São Paulo immediately after the Dempsey Cookhouse was up and running. In addition to these debuts, we had traveled to the Bahamas to renovate and reopen Dune, which had been damaged in a hurricane, and we had reopened my beloved JoJo after an interior overhaul. Even without the normal operations involved in running twelve Manhattan restaurants, this would be an uncommonly busy year. So opening two restaurants in the same *week,* restaurants that were literally on opposite sides of the planet, was simply a part of being prepared, *flexible,* and having a great team, with each member in his or her optimal position.

Why *do* I do it? I don't have to. I want to. And travel is one critical reason.

Travel is my primary source of inspiration. If I were to stop moving, I'd die as a chef. One of the primary ways I ensure regular travel is by opening restaurants—in Shanghai, Tokyo, Paris, Dubai, Hong Kong, the West Indies, and throughout the United States. This guarantees that I and many of my chefs will travel to Singapore two or three times a year, and South America, and Los Angeles. I do it for the continual immersions in new cultures, sourcing food there, getting to know new staff members.

I have two restaurants in Las Vegas. Both are steak houses (traditional ones!). I don't get inspiration from Vegas. But they're killing it. They do $42 million in sales between them. I've already told you how these percentages work—6 percent off the top, 10 to 15 percent off the bottom, which is traditionally 10 percent of sales—so how can I not?

But then there's Tokyo. Here is a restaurant serving a high-end *omakase* menu with fourteen seats. This is not Vegas. This will never make a lot of money. I do it because it ensures that I'll go to Tokyo four times a year, one of the most inspiring places on earth to me. I opened in Tokyo solely because *the place* inspires me and inspires my chefs. Inspiration alone is worth this particular venture.

And I open restaurants because, well, how can I say no? It's what I've been doing since 1980, when I first did it for Outhier. In the 1990s, I was among the first chefs in America to branch out internationally, after a late breakfast and a chance meeting in an elevator. In all this time I have launched more than seventy restaurants. So, it's second nature for me. It's not easy, and I always feel stress before the first day, but I've got a great team, with my chefs getting the kitchen up and running and, in the front of the house, my brother Philippe training the greeters and servers, along with Alex Wolf, who had been in Singapore for weeks by the time we arrived, hiring and training the front-of-the-house staff. We know how to do this.

Today, my office receives offers to open restaurants pretty much every day. I won't put one just anywhere—the space and the country and the partners all have to be right. All these opportunities exist for me because of the strength of my flagship. I learned this from watching my old boss and mentor Louis Outhier. He had restaurants throughout the world, and these kept him busy enough. He figured he didn't need to keep his original L'Oasis, which he'd opened in 1954. This proved to be a significant error. Once he closed the restaurant, in 1988, the offers to establish new restaurants stopped, and some hotels, such as the Drake in New York, no longer renewed their contracts. It was a lesson I took to heart.

You can't rest on your laurels. The only way to stay vibrant and alive in this industry is to continue to make things new. Always be pushing yourself. Your staff will follow.

Almost all my restaurants outside New York City are licensing agreements, and they account for 75 percent of our business; I'm not an owner in these. For me, a licensing agreement means that I design and light the restaurant, hire the staff, train the front and the back of the house, create the menu, and put my name on the restaurant. For this, I'm paid a percentage not only of the net profits but also of the gross profits—meaning that even if the restaurant doesn't succeed, I'm guaranteed some compensation for the considerable efforts on the part of myself and the team that travels ahead of me, and with me, and stays behind to make the opening happen and ensure the success of the restaurant. I also receive a signing bonus.

That said, I don't do this for the money. I never do anything for money alone. Do what you love and do it well and the money will come, and you will be happy.

Finally, but very importantly, I open new restaurants to create opportunities for my chefs, people who may want to live abroad for a time, chefs who want to see other parts of the world, and to allow my staff in New York to move up in the ranks. As all executive chefs and chefs de cuisine know, part of the key to success in this business is keeping a cohesive team and reducing turnover in the kitchen. This is not easy in a company comprising scores of restaurants and thousands of employees. The way you reduce turnover is to continually give your young chefs new opportunities within your company. One of the great and rewarding parts of being a chef is watching young chefs grow, people like Lois Freedman and Daniel Del Vecchio, and Pierre Schutz, executive chef at the Mark in Manhattan, who started with me way back in Boston, in 1985. These are the people who allow me to do what I can do.

*

THIS NEW RESTAURANT, the Dempsey Cookhouse, is in an airy former barracks along with two other restaurants, in a building with very high ceilings. Ours uses a black-and-white decor and the lush greenery of tropical plants around the perimeter and hanging above the bar. Unusually, it is not within a hotel. (Most of our licensing agreements are with large hotels, which have to have a food-service component.) Soon after I arrived in Singapore, I sat in the chairs of the Dempsey for the first time and felt like a king. The place has a colonial vibe that's appropriate to the city, and sitting there, I felt optimistic, knowing that if you create an atmosphere that's comfortable and engaging and offer food that's not available anywhere else, you will have a successful restaurant. My restaurant designer, Paola Navone, had done a fabulous job and would be joining us for the opening, putting her own finishing touches on the room.

The lighting—something so, so critical to a restaurant—had been created by Hervé Descottes, a genuine madman and a lighting guru. Hervé typically does projects of a different scale than a seventy-seat restaurant—lighting the Metropolitan Museum of Art's exterior, for instance, or the latest Frank Gehry construction. But ever since he handled Mercer Kitchen as part of his work for the Mercer Hotel, Hervé has lighted all my restaurants, as a favor to me and because he loves fine food and drink and being a part of this restaurant family. I looked forward to the arrival of my old friend.

My ace kitchen team was hard at work. Chef Tom McKenna had been leading the kitchen for weeks now, finding and training the new cooks. At his side had been Daniel Everts, a Scandinavian who ran my Dubai kitchen for several years and is now part of the traveling band, my culinary trainer and coordinator. Also in the kitchen was Magnus Hansson, another Scandinavian and a genius with bread dough; we would be doing all our own breads here.

In the front of the house, my director of restaurants, Alex Wolf, had been training the staff here; he would work closely with my brother to ensure a smooth opening.

How is it possible to launch five restaurants in one year? Philippe and Alex in front, Greg, Thomas, Daniel, and Sean in the kitchen, and Danny Del Vecchio overseeing both front and back. It's like putting together the Magnificent Seven—everybody does their job, and the opening goes beautifully. When they've finished their work here, they'll head to São Paulo, Brazil, and do it all over again. (With a Michelin star straight out of the gate, no less—thanks guys!) I've loved being part of a team ever since I began in this business.

*

BUT THERE ARE ALWAYS, always issues. Here at the Dempsey Cookhouse in Singapore, we have a pizza oven for the truffle and fontina pizza, but the chefs on this station are not up to speed. There are still issues on the sauté station and with getting the food out quickly and well, which is precisely why we have these friends-and-family dinners, dinners we don't charge for, as a way of giving our servers a chance to practice without fear of failing with paying guests. And we're also having problems getting good seafood—ironic, given that we're in Singapore, an island off the southern tip of the Malay Peninsula. The quality is not there, and my chefs are struggling to find purveyors who can supply the restaurant well and reliably. We're wondering where our American counterparts are getting theirs. Right now, here in Singapore, Daniel Boulud has a DB Bistro, and Nancy Silverton has opened Mozza. The Japanese-born Australian chef Tetsuya Wakuda has a sushi outpost here—presumably he's getting all his fish from nearby Japan. Sourcing great seafood, great everything, is one of the more difficult parts of opening restaurants in parts of the world that don't have the distribution infrastructure for great products that we do in America.

And my head chef has not even arrived.

Training the cooks is a major part of the opening. Printed prep lists for each station and recipes calculated to one hundredth of a gram can't account for all the variables cooks encounter on the line during a busy service. That is, cooking can't be reduced to a set of written instructions and amounts, neither on a restaurant's hot line or in a home kitchen. Half the cooking must be taught by doing and showing—there are many things a cook learns only by watching and doing, and doing over and over. This is why Thomas McKenna and Daniel Everts and Alex Wolf and the others arrived in Singapore a month before opening, and even a month is cutting it close for a brand-new staff in an unfamiliar kitchen, workers who don't know our kitchen culture.

So when we open the restaurant, even I will be on the line with Thomas and Greg and Daniel, teaching the new young chefs how I want the dishes.

One of our advantages is that so many of my dishes are so simple and, therefore, not particularly difficult for a young chef to execute. A longtime standard at Jean-Georges is on the opening menu, the Parmesan-crusted chicken. A chicken breast is floured, coated with a stiff egg-white meringue, dipped in a mixture of freshly grated Parmigiano-Reggiano, served with boiled artichokes and butter and lemon, and finished with basil. That's really it. The crust is fabulous. I combine finely grated Parmesan and thickly grated Parmesan so it's got an uneven texture. We mix some flour into this to help hold it together, and when it cooks, it will absorb the fat melting out of the cheese so you don't lose the fat. The egg white also helps it to get very crispy. That's it; serve it with boiled artichokes and some *beurre fondue,* butter whisked into lemon juice. Again, simplicity is all. There's no reason four-star cuisine needs to be complicated when you have the best ingredients.

And the service our first night there, just twelve hours after Philippe, Dan, Greg, Sean, and I stepped off the plane from New York, goes smoothly.

*

BECAUSE WE'D BEEN ABLE to sleep for most of the hours on the flights over and then worked our way through the afternoon jet lag, which always seems to hit at around three or four p.m. here, we were able to sleep all the way through that first night and get up early for a tour of the Geylang Serai Market with Eve Felder, managing director of the Culinary Institute of America's Singapore campus. Chef Felder had been extremely helpful in finding many of our staff members, and she wanted to show us the market.

Markets can tell you a lot about the culture you've entered, as I've said, and changes in markets you've known reflect broader cultural changes. I had not been to this market—whose name, Eve explained, translates to "lemongrass," because the area was once a lemongrass farm—which caters to the Muslim and Peranakan communities. Peranakan is the blended tradition created when Chinese sailing explorations of the fifteenth, sixteenth, and seventeenth centuries brought settlers to Malaysia and Indonesia. It's a great example of why I find this part of the world so endlessly fascinating and inspiring, the diversity of cultures here. The people here celebrate this diversity, this melting pot of Chinese, Indian, Malaysian, Muslim, and Indonesian cultures. And, of course, their food is a similar stew. Because this market also caters to Muslim communities, you'll find no pork here. For pork you have to go to the Chinese market a few blocks down the road.

Here you'll find stalls selling numerous chili blends and curries. And stalls selling the local fruits, including many varieties of bananas—naturally ripened ones, unlike what's available in North America—and jackfruit, durian, and dragon fruit, as well as greens, and rhizomes and aromatics (fresh turmeric, galangal, lemongrass). There are also stalls for lamb, beef, and chicken, plus aisles and aisles of fish purveyors. The fish is not exactly sushi grade—they have virtually no refrigeration here. Though we did buy some octopus with hopes that it would be more tender than what our current purveyor had brought us. (And so it turned out to be!)

But invariably I'm most excited by the street food—"hawker food," as it's called here. I've always found this kind of food to be the most dynamic and inspirational segment of any culture's food scene. And the hawker food of the Geylang Serai Market didn't disappoint. I was fascinated by the vendors' techniques with dough. The first food stand Eve brought us to was one preparing roti, a form of flatbread that, here, is stretched thin as a crepe, so that the elastic dough is nearly as tender as a crepe, and it does what a crepe does: it serves as a container for other ingredients. The vendor spread the dough, big as a manhole cover, onto his flattop, cracked whole eggs onto it, folded the edges over to contain the egg, and kept folding as it cooked, until the dough was the size of a small, thin envelope. A perfect breakfast. *Dosai* (or *thosai*) are made from a fermented batter of rice and lentils spread on a griddle and cooked till it's crispy. This batter sticks to the griddle, and as it browns, it peels away from the griddle into a large wafer-thin sheet that you can break pieces from to dip in a variety of condiments. We do a version of this at the new vegetarian restaurant in Manhattan, ABCV, and it was great to see it done here, so huge and crispy, a display of the Indian culture that had found its way to Singapore.

The most fascinating dough technique we saw was the one used to make *popiah*, spring roll wrappers. *Popiah* dough combines the qualities of both the stretchy wheat dough used for the roti and the *dosai* dough, with its propensity for sticking to a griddle. A large ball of the sticky dough is rubbed in a circular motion on the griddle—and a thin layer of it sticks to the griddle when the ball of dough is lifted up. When this cooks, it peels away from the steel, leaving the thinnest of wrappers, stiff but pliable. These can be filled, rolled, and fried, and you'll find them all over this part of Asia. Watching such local cooking demonstrations is one of the thousand ways a chef educates him- or herself.

*

TWO WEEKS BEFORE we opened the Dempsey Cookhouse, we didn't have a chef, or even any candidates, and this made me so nervous. I asked all my guys if they knew anyone, and Daniel Everts, who had run the Jean-Georges Dubai kitchen, said he had a friend in Stockholm who might be interested. Daniel contacted the friend, Erik Gustafsson, told him there was an opening, and Erik said he was interested.

We sent Erik to Singapore, he did some cooking for the team, and my guys there said he was fantastic. So I got him on the phone, talked to him a little, and liked him. I asked him, "What are you doing right now?"

We flew him to New York to talk further, interview, and cook. I still liked him. I asked him to cook one of my Jean-Georges dishes, my scallops with the caper-raisin emulsion, and also a dish that meant something to him. For the latter, he chose a canapé with potato, bleak roe (a Swedish caviar), pickled onion, dill, and a variation of mushrooms with pickled kohlrabi, onion royale, and some fresh herbs.

He cooked well, and at last I had my chef for Singapore.

But now we were about to open, and he wasn't here. He'd returned to Stockholm to tie up some loose ends and prepare for his job in Singapore. I thought he'd be here by now, only by the time we got back to the restaurant, I discovered that he was still en route and wouldn't arrive until after the friends-and-family service. Still, he would make it in time to sit at a table with my opening chefs to have his first meal at the Dempsey Cookhouse, some fantastic John Dory we'd sourced, roasted whole on the bone. His first day on the job would be opening day of the restaurant.

*

THE NEXT MORNING at breakfast, I heard Greg say what the main order of the day was: "To get the executive chef up to speed." He sighed and raised his eyebrows. "Our executive chef is currently the least-informed person in the kitchen."

That was cutting it close. This had never happened before. We had brought in Erik to run the restaurant, and now we were about to throw forty-five new recipes at him in an unfamiliar kitchen with a completely new staff and say, "We open in eight hours, and you're in charge!"

But my opening team and I would stay beside him for a week to make sure he got up to speed quickly. He was calm and focused, and I could tell within the first hour that he was completely capable of running this kitchen. You really do know right away in a kitchen, within the first hour of working with someone, what they're capable of, how well they'll fit in. Kitchens and cooking are like this—it's such a physical place, the kitchen, that deficits are quickly revealed. You can't hide in a kitchen, can't cover things up. If you lie to yourself, it becomes obvious to everyone almost immediately.

But that's also part of the nature of *our* kitchens—this ability to train a team and get a new staff, a new chef in

gear in a short time. We're not a fear kitchen. Many kitchens I know, often high-end kitchens, are fear kitchens. And
I understand this, but I've never been a part of one, and I
don't believe it's the best way to go. It's easier, that's for
sure—fear is the quickest way to get results from your staff.
Fear motivates, no doubt about that. But it's not for the best
in the long term. Your staff won't be happy; they'll become
frustrated in a fear kitchen. You'll lose people. In the end,
fear is an unsustainable method of motivating workers.

You can scare people, and the work will get done fast,
but soon they'll leave, or they'll never develop the way
they might have. Or you can have a little more patience
with them, which slows everything down, but over time,
these cooks will develop more soundly and solidly than
they would have had they been in a fear kitchen. They'll be
more satisfied with their work, and it will be meaningful to
them. When you end a fifteen-hour workday with a sense
of satisfaction, rather than relief that it's done and that the
threat is gone, you get better at what you're trying to do,
and you progress more quickly. The work is hard either
way. One cook feels good about his work; the other dreads
going to work in the morning. It makes a difference.

My hope in all my kitchens is to create a culture of positive mentorship. This is what's best, both for the young
cooks and for the mentors, as well as for the business. It
makes sense, no? To mentor cooks in what is a very hard
profession, teach them, *feed* them so that they can grow,
instead of cracking the whip. It requires more effort on the
part of the people training and managing the staff; those
in charge have to take on the role of mentor. But as with

everything else, the extra effort up front brings great dividends in the end.

The front of the house is no different. It's all one team.

*

TWO DAYS AFTER we landed in Singapore, it was opening day. Paying customers arrived, we were in business, and Erik did fine. The service was slow, inevitably. This work requires repetition. We offered a tasting menu, and half the customers ordered it. The kitchen got buried, and so I decided to cancel that menu; this eliminated some dishes and simplified the timing for all of the stations. Just one à la carte menu was plenty. I discovered that everyone was ordering the expensive caviar. This was what had happened at the friends-and-family meals, but I'd assumed it was simply that because no one was paying for the food, they were ordering the luxury items. Not so. Everyone wanted the luxury items here in Singapore. We offered four pizzas, but the only one ordered was the truffle pizza. Interesting.

Also, there was a strong call for lamb. Initially I'd put a pork chop on the menu, but I'd quickly replaced it with lamb. Great lamb is available from New Zealand, to the south of Singapore, lamb that grazes on salty grasses near the ocean, and it is delicious. We grill the chops and finish them with a passion fruit barbecue glaze. Amazing.

Over the course of the year, however, the menu would change considerably, based on what people ordered, what products were available to the chef. You have to be flexible. I eliminated the caviar with lemon gelée and crème fraîche. A tasting menu of three items was enough. We removed the crab dumplings, which I loved but which sold only so-so—pepper crab is a staple here, and even a reimagining of the dish didn't interest people so familiar with it. Instead, to show off the delicious crab, we created a crab toast. We changed the chicken to one with a habanero hot sauce, replaced the pork chop with the lamb. And we took the salmon off and put on sea trout, with coconut milk and basil, because the quality of this trout was so much better than the salmon we could get here.

We opened on a Friday, and by Monday it was almost like a different restaurant, it was running so smoothly. Christina Ong, who develops luxury and lifestyle hotel and retail properties such as this one, was happy with us. I think she was impressed that we sent such a large team to stay for so long to open the restaurant: more than a dozen professionals, encompassing both the front and the back of the house, for a total of six weeks of support.

"I'm opening a hotel in Bali in November," Christina called to me from across the dining room as we were setting up one afternoon. "I'd love to have you there!"

"Whoa," I said. "Let's get this one off the ground first!"

But it pleased me that she'd offered. And besides, we needed to head to Brazil, to open in São Paulo after this.

It was proving to be a banner year. The Dempsey made a wonderful addition to our fleet of restaurants not in hotels (the others were Mercato, in both Shanghai and Guangzhou, and JG kitchens in Tokyo and in Dubai). I was so proud to have a team that could head back across the world, to the opposite hemisphere, to open in São Paulo. From there they would travel to London to open at the Connaught. And two more restaurants in New York would follow in quick succession: Public Kitchen, at the Public hotel, soon after the opening of ABCV, and then Rooftop Beverly Hills at the Waldorf in Los Angeles. Moreover, the people from Los Angeles restaurant ate at ABCV and began clamoring for these original vegetarian and vegan dishes and an ABCV Los Angeles. These debuts were in addition to reopening Dune in the Bahamas and Jean-Georges Steakhouse in Las Vegas. All of the parts of the business feed new businesses, new launches. But we can do it because we are a team; everyone has their job, their forte.

And finally, in the fall, toward the very end of the year, we had one more special opening. JoJo reopened after a complete overhaul, bringing a clean, modern decor to the two-story restaurant, the place where I'd begun my career as an independent chef-restaurateur, twenty-six years and dozens of restaurants later.

*

IN MARCH 2017, just back from Singapore and three days after my sixtieth birthday, we had a party at the restaurant Jean-Georges to celebrate its twentieth anniversary.

The place was packed. A band played. Servers poured wines and champagne. Greg and Mark oversaw the kitchen, sending out plate after plate of canapés—beggars' purses filled with caviar and adorned with gold leaf, more caviar topping a small egg yolk grilled sandwich, shrimp satays and beef skewers and samosas and truffled endive salad in a baby endive leaf. Eight thousand canapés for more that four hundred guests, including my mother and my siblings, my children, so many friends, such as Hervé, my lighting genius, other New York restaurateurs, chefs of my generation, Daniel Boulud and Alfred Portale, and younger chefs, so many of whom had worked for me at Jean-Georges, such as Wylie Dufresne, Johnny Iuzzini, too many to name.

Birthdays and anniversaries are a time for celebration and also reflection. Sixty is a big birthday, and so was sixteen. I never forget that it was on this birthday that my father took me to Auberge de l'Ill, the gift that would direct my life.

I've had a lucky life. I don't know how to account for it other than that. Luck and hard work. I've been successful in work at every stage. Life hasn't been without pain, but I've suffered no tragedies. Losing my father was difficult, but he was in his eighties; his death wasn't sudden, and of course it is our hope and prayer to outlive our parents. I've been divorced twice—and this is never happy. I've suffered only one extremely negative review, in which I felt personally attacked, but that pain went away with time. And I've had to close two restaurants I cared about. Closing down is hardest for the teams that run the restaurant and so is especially unhappy for me because of that.

But these are small bumps in a long road. A negative review and two restaurant closings, losing a Michelin star at my flagship—these are truly the worst I've suffered, so you can understand how at age sixty, looking back on my life, I can say I feel nothing but good fortune. I worked hard at every step. I've really only taken off two days in the past two years—that's how connected I am to the restaurants. And it's not as if, when I get a text from someone at one of the restaurants, it's work. I feel more that I'm getting a text from a friend. And I am. So, while I'm able to go home and leave my work behind me, there really is no dividing line between my work and my personal life.

I'm a manual person. I love action. I don't overthink—if I did that the way I see some people do, I'd be dead already. I tell my chefs, I tell my kids, If you get stuck, move on, don't dwell on things. Always be looking ahead, always be moving forward. But on this birthday and anniversary, I am looking back. Twenty-four years after that meal at Auberge, almost to the day, I opened my flagship restaurant. And twenty years after opening it, today, at this sixtieth birthday party, it remains a strong business and—I am grateful for this—one of Manhattan's premier restaurants, one of five restaurants holding four *New York Times'* stars. And I could only do this, all of this, because of my team.

Molten Chocolate Cake

I conclude with something sweet. One of the most copied desserts in the country, I'm guessing—and it's an honor the cake has been on so many menus— happened unintentionally. I can't say I was the first to create a chocolate sponge cake with a liquid center. Michel Bras had been doing one for years. For his, you first had to make a ganache, then you made the batter, then you put them together. Other chefs achieve a similar effect by making a soufflé and pouring in warm chocolate ganache tableside, another classic preparation that gives you a similar effect. But that, too, requires two separate preparations. I create mine in one step: one batter, five or six minutes in the oven, and that's it—so simple, and every bit as delicious and fun to eat as the others.

Here's how it happened. The year was 1987 or 1988, at Restaurant Lafayette. We were doing a huge wedding at the hotel above the restaurant, five hundred people. The wedding couple had come in to discuss the menu and taste the food we would be serving, and my pastry chef, who'd come from Outhier, Jean-Marc Burillier, made them, at the last minute, a simple chocolate sponge. He started with butter and sugar whipped to ribbons, with just a little bit of flour. This mixture was then whipped into chocolate and butter melted to a ganache consistency, then poured into four molds and popped it in the oven for ten minutes. We served these warm, traditional cakes to the couple. They loved it.

The night of the party, I oversaw the dinner part of the banquet. When that was over, I went downstairs to the Lafayette kitchen to continue the evening's restaurant service. About twenty minutes later, one of the waiters serving at the banquet ran down to me. He'd seen people cutting into their cakes and the egg-based cake batter running out onto the plate. "Chef!" he said, "We've just served five hundred chocolate cakes that are raw in the center!"

"F——!" I said, slapping my forehead, and bolted upstairs. I knew exactly what had happened. It was just like those chickens I'd had to cook at the family meal all those years ago as an apprentice for Monsieur Paul at Auberge. You put four small cakes in an oven, they bake properly. You jam five hundred cakes into all the oven space you have, and the temperature drops. Those cakes *were* raw in the center.

By the time I got to the banquet hall and looked around, people were eating every bit. They were all but licking their plates. Everyone . . . *loved* it.

I addressed the crowd and talked about all the courses they'd had. When I got to the end, I mentioned the . . . "molten chocolate cake." When I described it, I received a standing ovation.

I put the dish on the Lafayette menu the next day, and we've been serving it since.

1 stick (4 ounces) unsalted butter, cut into four pieces, plus a little for buttering the molds
4 ounces bittersweet chocolate, preferably Valrhona, broken into pieces

Preheat your oven to 450°F.

Combine the chocolate and the butter in a saucier pan. I set the saucier pan in a second saucier pan, half filled with water, to make an impromptu double boiler, but use a standard double boiler if you wish, to allow the gentle heat to melt the two ingredients.

2 eggs
2 egg yolks
¼ cup sugar
2 teaspoons flour, plus a little more for dusting

While the chocolate is melting, butter four molds—we use 4-ounce brioche molds, but ramekins are fine as well—and flour them, shaking out the excess flour.

Combine the eggs, egg yolks, sugar, and 2 teaspoons of flour and whip the mixture till it becomes thick and falls in ribbons.

By now the chocolate and butter should be nearly melted—whisk them together till you have a lovely ganache, still very warm. Slowly beat the egg-sugar mixture into the chocolate. When the ingredients are smoothly incorporated, set your molds on a sheet tray and divide the mixture among your molds. Put the tray in the oven. Bake them for 6 minutes. Pull them out and have a look. The edges should be set, but the center should be indented and a little wobbly. This is perfect. If you think the center is too fluid, return the tray to the oven for another minute.

The good thing about this dish is that if you go too far, you wind up with a delicious brownie-like cake—it's got so much butter it will never be dry—so mistakes on either end are fine!

SERVES 4

This may be the dish I'm most famous for. My pastry chef's error! Unquestionably, it's the best *à la minute* dessert you can offer guests, hands down. You can make the batter ahead of time, pour it into molds, and refrigerate them. Be sure to remove them a good hour before you want to cook them so they come to room temperature. They'll still be good, though when you make them ahead, they tend to be a little denser. Made *à la minute* (you can melt the chocolate and butter and whip the eggs ahead of time if you wish), these cakes are an extraordinary dessert. No matter what you've served for dinner, this is what your guests will be remarking on. Serve it simply, with a scoop of vanilla ice cream. It's the best.

A spearfisherman, Alan Brown, caught this
strawberry grouper in the Bahamas for my restaurant
Dune. How I love to be near the water.

EPILOGUE

WHEN MY OLDEST CHILD, CÉDRIC, WHO WAS BORN WHILE I was becoming a chef in Bangkok, came to me to say he wanted to become a chef, I told him, "*No*. Being a chef, it's no kind of life."

But he persisted in his desire, went to culinary school, and is now a key member of my team, executive chef of Perry St., in Manhattan's West Village.

I meant what I told Cédric with all my heart. It's a hard, hard life. And this comes from a chef who, by appearances, has made it all look easy, who has had nothing but good luck and good fortune all along the way. And still it's a continuous struggle.

*

IN THE END, if you will be a chef, there are only a few things you need to know in order to learn the rest. Cleanliness, again, is the first essential. Cleanliness in the way you look, in the way you think—*focused*. Clean in the way you carry yourself. In the way you keep your station. In the way you cook.

Number two: a knowledge of food is something you build over time, and the more you know, the more successful you stand to be. One of the many great facets of being a chef is that you're always learning. You learn every day you work. You learn when you travel. I'd never seen the making of the spring roll wrappers as I did in Singapore just recently. And you also learn by working with a broad spectrum of cooks.

As we planned the opening of ABCV, considering different menu ideas and testing dishes, we had a number of thoughts about using chickpeas. One day in the kitchen we had a lot of chickpea cooking liquid. One of the chefs called it "aquafaba" and asked if we knew what we could do with it. If you've been cooking vegan for any time at all, you likely know about aquafaba, but I'd never heard the term. Our young cook put some of this cooled cooking liquid in a bowl and began whipping it. In no time she had a beautiful meringue. It whipped up just like egg whites. I thought it was amazing, and we quickly put the aquafaba to use in place of egg-white meringue in our chocolate mousse, so that now we have a vegan version of this popular dish every bit as good as a traditional mousse. Who knows what other ways this new ingredient will work its way onto the menu. I was sixty and still learning. I love it.

So the first component of knowledge is a comprehensive understanding of the food itself. The second component is a knowledge of fundamental cooking techniques. And here you don't necessarily keep learning new things as you learn about food itself; rather, you continuously deepen your knowledge of techniques and continue to refine your techniques. A carpenter's joints always get tighter, and a cook's fundamental techniques grow ever more graceful and refined.

The third quality all great chefs share is extraordinary discipline. This extends to all areas of your life, but it's visible in chefs in their cleanliness and comportment. Is your uniform immaculate, is your station wiped down, is the floor at your station as clean as your counter? Can you maintain this discipline at the end of a fourteen-hour day at the end of a six-day week? It's something that must be developed early and maintained and enhanced throughout your career.

Cleanliness, knowledge of food and technique, and personal discipline.

And the final quality of a chef who will be successful, the hardest component of all to teach, is the desire to *serve,* the many forms of it, of hospitality. It's difficult to teach because true hospitality comes from within. It's simply the desire to make people happy, to know what they want before they know they're going to want it. This is the sense of serving—the chef's sixth sense. I'd been using it since I was a boy, planning my siblings' parties.

I think most people have this urge to some degree. We like to make our family and friends happy, to please them. It's easy to cook at home for friends. But if you are a true cook, you cook for sixty, for eighty, for one hundred people, mostly people you don't know. You have to want to please strangers every bit as much as you want to please your family and friends.

And you must create in all the people you serve the desire to return for more. I tell my staff that the people who are already returning customers, regulars—these people are easy to please. I made them. With exciting food and great service. Now it's your turn. You. You make some new regulars, make your own. Touch them, talk to them, meet their needs, please them.

Like Charlie Cissel. He was behind the bar on day one of Jean-Georges, and he's there today. He has made his own regulars. I've seen some people enter the restaurant, ask for Charlie, and, finding that he's off that night, leave. That's an amazing server. The one who makes you feel at home.

That's the biggest intangible in whether or not a chef will be successful—the desire to serve.

Some have it, and some, you can see, need more coaxing. One chef who worked for me, Mike Ramos, had a good palate but was no good on the line. All my chefs de cuisine wanted to get rid of him. But I saw something in him. I had the patience to work with him and push the clouds away. I didn't always have patience with everyone. But he just needed a little more time to get his physical coordination aligned with his thoughts and his palate. And he turned out to be a great cook.

Of course, many come with all kinds of passion and dreams but have no idea how hard the work actually is, and they do not succeed. And no amount of coaxing can bring out what is not there to begin with.

Others, as I've said, I had no clue about what they had in them. Daniel Humm was on the meat station here at Jean-Georges for a year and a half. Kept his head down and just worked. Then he left Jean-Georges and led Eleven Madison Park and the NoMad to renown and Michelin stars, and he is now one of the best chefs in the country. Wylie

Dufresne worked garde-manger here as well. Who could have predicted that he would become one of the most talented avant-garde chefs in the world at WD-50? These chefs had that spark in them from the beginning. They used the Jean-Georges kitchen to nurture it.

Ultimately, it's up to you, what passion and drive you bring to the work. The passion and drive you bring to your growing knowledge of food, your deepening physical mastery of cooking techniques, your discipline, and your desire to serve.

The growing prominence of chefs, the increasing interest in cooking, the focus on restaurants of higher and higher quality—these things have resulted in *kitchens* of increasingly higher quality. There is more decorum, more professionalism in restaurant kitchens than ever before in the history of restaurants, and there are better working conditions, too. I think it's actually easier for cooks today than it was when I was growing up. Cooks work fewer hours and often receive benefits. Also, remember that this country's population will continue to grow—so there will always be room for more restaurants. You will always have work and you will *always* be well fed. But "easier" is a relative term. The work of a chef remains intense, the hours long. It is unrelenting. And I will still advise my grandkids to pursue other work. The life of a chef is so hard that I will say to them, "It's no kind of life."

But if I *can't* persuade them and they are determined to follow the path of the chef, I will then tell them this: If you embrace it with all that you have and all that you are, there is potentially no more rewarding work than that of the chef, the work of feeding people, the work of serving.

ACKNOWLEDGMENTS

LOOKING BACK ON MY LIFE, I HAVE MANY PEOPLE TO thank, but I can't begin any other way than by thanking my parents, Jeanine and Georges Vongerichten. My father, who died at age seventy-nine, cooked almost every Sunday meal our family shared throughout my youth, and he gave me the meal that directed my life. My mother, who still makes pounds of foie gras at Christmas, my beloved baeckeoffe, and drives to buy her daily baguette, cooked every other meal, for dozens of people every day. She was truly my first mentor. I love you Mom. Thank you.

Grandma Matilde and Aunt Lucie, who lived with us, fed my two brothers, my sister, and me in the morning and took care of us while my parents worked. I'm lucky for all my siblings, my older sister, Martine, and my younger brothers, Christian and Philippe. Philippe arrived in 1990 to help me open JoJo and never left, and I am a lucky man to have him. He's an extraordinary host at Jean-Georges, a teacher of restaurant service, a key member of our team. I barely knew him growing up, our ages were so far apart—

but how lucky I am that he has become such an integral part of my life.

Chef Paul Haeberlin, of Auberge de l'Ill, gave me my first job, and during a three-year apprenticeship taught me the precision that would allow me to travel anywhere. His brother, Jean-Pierre, was both a visual artist and director of the restaurant. I learned hospitality and elegance in the dining room by watching him.

Louis Outhier, chef of the 3-star L'Oasis, is the man who most influenced my career, not only by teaching me extraordinary à la minute cooking but, more significantly, by asking a twenty-three-year-old *chef de partie* to open a restaurant in Bangkok for him. I was too scared at the time to think about it, but looking back, he put an extraordinary amount of trust in me with that decision, and I am forever grateful. I would ultimately open ten restaurants for him around the world, the last of which brought me to New York. That first restaurant was in the Oriental hotel, where Bruno Schöpfer was the food and beverage director of the hotel. The executive chef was Norbert Kostner. Both were instrumental in teaching me how hotels and food service worked at that level—lessons on food and labor cost, something I, having only worked as *commis* and *chef de partie* in four Michelin 3-star restaurants, knew nothing about. I didn't know it then, but they were teaching me how to be a chef, not a cook.

My third restaurant, after two years with Outhier, was Restaurant Paul Bocuse. How can anyone say enough about this man, master of masters? No chef did more for our industry than he. Bocuse brought chefs out of the kitchen and into the light, forever changing our profession and paving the way for all chefs to take culinary arts to new heights.

Eckart Witzigmann was the chef at my fourth restaurant, Tantris. When I went to work for him at age twenty-two, he was the youngest chef, and first German chef, to have earned 3 Michelin stars. From him I learned how to cook under pressure, as well as diligence and imagination (he would post a completely new menu daily a couple hours before service—pressure!).

At Lafayette in the Drake Hotel in Manhattan, I met my spiritual father, Phil Suarez. Phil was the second man to put enormous trust in me by depositing $250,000 in an escrow account, for whenever I was ready to open my own place. I quickly was, opening JoJo, and Phil and I have remained partners and deep friends ever since. He even got me my green card. I am forever in his debt.

There are too many staff members to thank individually. I am blessed by an extraordinary staff, all of whom force me to raise my own bar daily. I must call out some of them: first, the Original Gangsters of New York, with me from Lafayette to this day—Pierre Schultz, now Executive Chef of the Mark Hotel; Ron Gallo, CDC of The Inn at Pound Ridge; Lois Freedman, president of Jean-Georges Management; and Hanh Vinh Tu, whom I found in a Vietnamese refugee center downtown in the 1980s, and is now a line cook at The Mercer Kitchen.

I could not be a restaurateur without great *chefs de cuisine*, such as Mark Lapico, who runs the kitchen of my flagship restaurant, Jean-Georges, as well as Nougatine; Kristen Snavely, ABC Kitchen; Camila Avendano, ABC Cocina; Neil Harden, ABCV; Steven Boutross, JoJo;

Thomas McKenna, Louis/Public Kitchen; Chris Beischer, The Mercer Kitchen; Drew Hiatt, Topping Rose House; Noah Poses, The Fulton; Amy Trevino, Paris Café and Lisbon Lounge; Rob Moore, Prime Steakhouse; Sean Griffin, Jean-Georges Steakhouse; Nikolai Grigorov, Jean-Georges Shanghai; Kelvin Chai, Mercato Shanghai; Sebastien Heslot, Market Paris; Stuart Roger, Suviche and Seared; Lester Dean, Dune; Mathieu Fernandez, Sand Bar; Hamide Suuctugu, Matador Room; Alex Powell, Market Miami; Melissa Revilla, Dempsey Cookhouse and Bar; Felipe Rodriques, Jean-Georges Sao Paolo; Joseph Castro, Jean-Georges Beverly Hills; Thuy Vo, Rooftop by JG; Anshu Anghotra, Jean-Georges at The Connaught; Alex Huang, Mercato Guangzhou; Ton Mochizuki, Jean-Georges Tokyo; Nicholas Ugliarolo, Jean-Georges Philadelphia.

Gregory Brainin is our Director of Culinary Development, an ingenious and talented cook in charge of the food. In charge of all restaurants is Daniel Del Vecchio, Executive Vice President who began as a grill cook at Vong in the 1990s. I'd be lost without him. And without Lina Varriale, my executive assistant.

I am more grateful than I can say for my three children: Chloe, my youngest; Louise, my second born; and Cédric, the eldest, who are following in my footsteps even though I did not want them to! Chloe helps out as a hostess during summer recess, Louise runs Food Dreams, our foundation that helps underprivileged kids get access to culinary educations. Cédric is chef of the restaurant Perry Street, Vong Kitchen in Jakarta, and the new Wayan in Soho. And finally, thanks to the future, my grandchildren, Olivier, Noah, and Miran.

*

Michael Ruhlman and JGV would like to thank Maria Guarnaschelli, who initiated this project at W. W. Norton, and Melanie Tortoroli, who carried it through. Thanks also to the excellent team at Norton, including Susan Sanfrey, Will Scarlett, and Anna Oler, and to copyeditor Bonnie Thompson and proofreader Lynne Cannon Menges.